KUM◯N®
MATH. READING. SUCCESS.

P9-DEC-040

What is Kumon?

Kumon is the world's largest supplemental education provider and a leader in producing outstanding results. After-school programs in math and reading at Kumon Centers around the globe have been helping children succeed for 50 years.

Kumon Workbooks represent just a fraction of our complete curriculum of preschool-to-college-level material assigned at Kumon Centers under the supervision of trained Kumon Instructors.

The Kumon Method enables each child to progress successfully by practicing material until concepts are mastered and advancing in small, manageable increments. Instructors carefully assign materials and pace advancement according to the strengths and needs of each individual student.

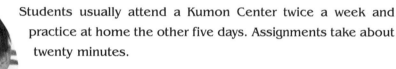

Students usually attend a Kumon Center twice a week and practice at home the other five days. Assignments take about twenty minutes.

Kumon helps students of all ages and abilities master the basics, improve concentration and study habits, and build confidence.

How did Kumon begin?

IT ALL BEGAN IN JAPAN 50 YEARS AGO when a parent and teacher named Toru Kumon found a way to help his son Takeshi do better in school. At the prompting of his wife, he created a series of short assignments that his son could complete successfully in less than 20 minutes a day and that would ultimately make high school math easy. Because each was just a bit more challenging than the last, Takeshi was able to master the skills and gain the confidence to keep advancing.

This unique self-learning method was so successful that Toru's son was able to do calculus by the time he was in the sixth grade. Understanding the value of good reading comprehension, Mr. Kumon then developed a reading program employing the same method. His programs are the basis and inspiration of those offered at Kumon Centers today under the expert guidance of professional Kumon Instructors.

Mr. Toru Kumon
Founder of Kumon

What can Kumon do for my child?

Kumon is geared to children of all ages and skill levels. Whether you want to give your child a leg up in his or her schooling, build a strong foundation for future studies or address a possible learning problem, Kumon provides an effective program for developing key learning skills given the strengths and needs of each individual child.

What makes Kumon so different?

Kumon uses neither a classroom model nor a tutoring approach. It's designed to facilitate self-acquisition of the skills and study habits needed to improve academic performance. This empowers children to succeed on their own, giving them a sense of accomplishment that fosters further achievement. Whether for remedial work or enrichment, a child advances according to individual ability and initiative to reach his or her full potential. Kumon is not only effective, but also surprisingly affordable.

What is the role of the Kumon Instructor?

Kumon Instructors regard themselves more as mentors or coaches than teachers in the traditional sense. Their principal role is to provide the direction, support and encouragement that will guide the student to performing at 100% of his or her potential. Along with their rigorous training in the Kumon Method, all Kumon Instructors share a passion for education and an earnest desire to help children succeed.

KUMON FOSTERS:

- A mastery of the basics of reading and math
- Improved concentration and study habits
- Increased self-discipline and self-confidence
- A proficiency in material at every level
- Performance to each student's full potential
- A sense of accomplishment

▶▶ GETTING STARTED IS EASY. Just call us at 877.586.6671 or visit kumon.com to request our free brochure and find a Kumon Center near you. We'll direct you to an Instructor who will be happy to speak with you about how Kumon can address your child's particular needs and arrange a free placement test. There are more than 1,700 Kumon Centers in the U.S. and Canada, and students may enroll at any time throughout the year, even summer. Contact us today.

FIND OUT MORE ABOUT KUMON MATH & READING CENTERS.
Receive a free copy of our parent guide, *Every Child an Achiever,* by visiting
kumon.com/go.survey or calling 877.586.6671

Practicing Numbers
1 to 100

To parents Your child will first review the numbers 1-100 before being introduced to coins and their values. If your child encounters difficulty with this section, try some extended practice with numbers before continuing.

■ Say each number aloud while tracing it.

1	2	3	4	5	6	7	8	9	10
11	12	13	14	15	16	17	18	19	20
21	22	23	24	25	26	27	28	29	30
31	32	33	34	35	36	37	38	39	40
41	42	43	44	45	46	47	48	49	50
51	52	53	54	55	56	57	58	59	60
61	62	63	64	65	66	67	68	69	70
71	72	73	74	75	76	77	78	79	80
81	82	83	84	85	86	87	88	89	90
91	92	93	94	95	96	97	98	99	100

1

■Say each number aloud while tracing it.

1	2	3	4	5	6	7	8	9	10
11	12	13	14	15	16	17	18	19	20
21	22	23	24	25	26	27	28	29	30
31	32	33	34	35	36	37	38	39	40
41	42	43	44	45	46	47	48	49	50
51	52	53	54	55	56	57	58	59	60
61	62	63	64	65	66	67	68	69	70
71	72	73	74	75	76	77	78	79	80
81	82	83	84	85	86	87	88	89	90
91	92	93	94	95	96	97	98	99	100

Practicing Numbers
1 to 100

Name	
Date	

■ Say each number aloud while tracing it.

1	2	3	4	5	6	7	8	9	10
11	12	13	14	15	16	17	18	19	20
21	22	23	24	25	26	27	28	29	30
31	32	33	34	35	36	37	38	39	40
41	42	43	44	45	46	47	48	49	50
51	52	53	54	55	56	57	58	59	60
61	62	63	64	65	66	67	68	69	70
71	72	73	74	75	76	77	78	79	80
81	82	83	84	85	86	87	88	89	90
91	92	93	94	95	96	97	98	99	100

■Say each number aloud while writing it.

1	2	3	4	5	6	7	8	9	10
11	12	13	14	15	16	17	18	19	20
21	22	23	24	25	26	27	28	29	30
31	32	33	34	35	36	37	38	39	40
41	42	43	44	45	46	47	48	49	50
51	52	53	54	55	56	57	58	59	60
61	62	63	64	65	66	67	68	69	70
71	72	73	74	75	76	77	78	79	80
81	82	83	84	85	86	87	88	89	90
91	92	93	94	95	96	97	98	99	100

3 Introducing Coins
The Penny

Name

Date

To parents Now that your child has practiced the numbers from 1–100, he or she will be introduced to each coin worth less than a dollar. Try getting some pocket change out to help with these exercises.

penny

Front

1¢

Back

1¢

■ Add the value of each row of coins. Then trace the amount in the box on the right.

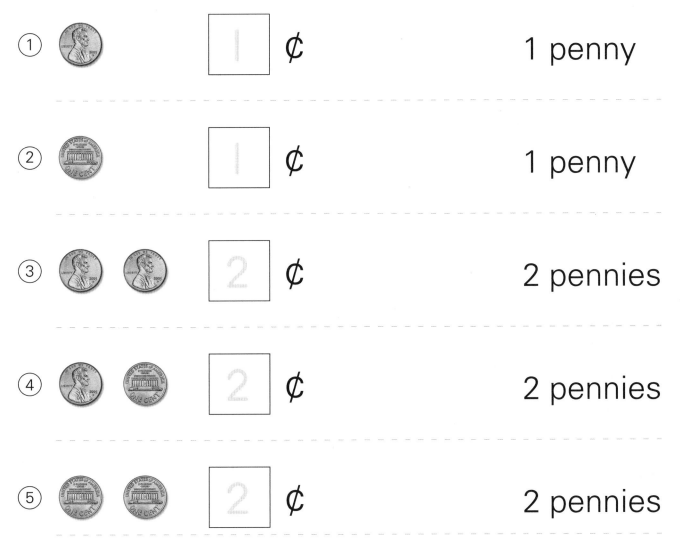

① |1| ¢   1 penny

② |1| ¢   1 penny

③ |2| ¢   2 pennies

④ |2| ¢   2 pennies

⑤ |2| ¢   2 pennies

Add the value of each row of coins. Then trace the amount in the box on the right.

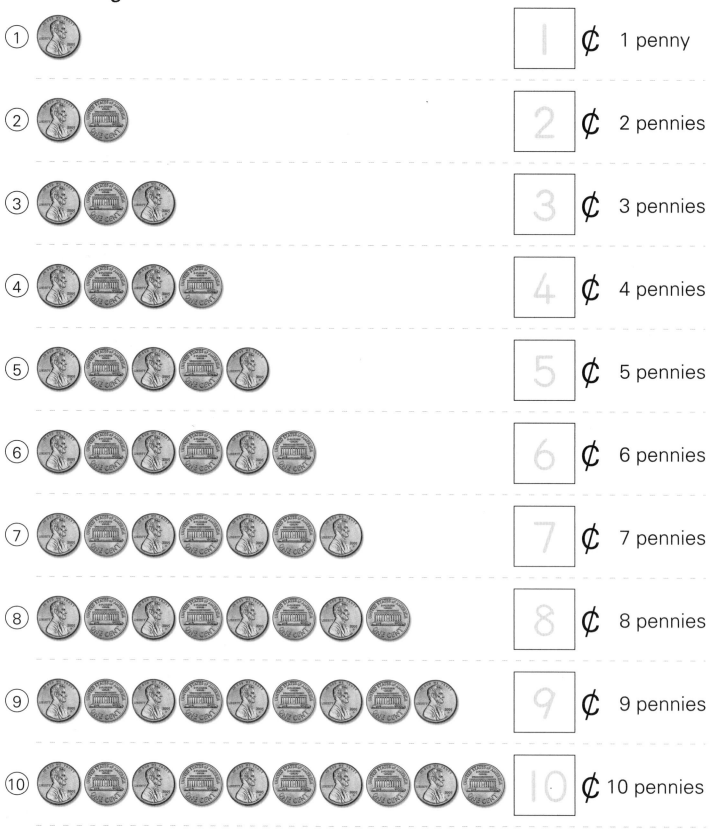

1. | 1 | ¢ 1 penny
2. | 2 | ¢ 2 pennies
3. | 3 | ¢ 3 pennies
4. | 4 | ¢ 4 pennies
5. | 5 | ¢ 5 pennies
6. | 6 | ¢ 6 pennies
7. | 7 | ¢ 7 pennies
8. | 8 | ¢ 8 pennies
9. | 9 | ¢ 9 pennies
10. | 10 | ¢ 10 pennies

Counting Coins
1¢ to 10¢

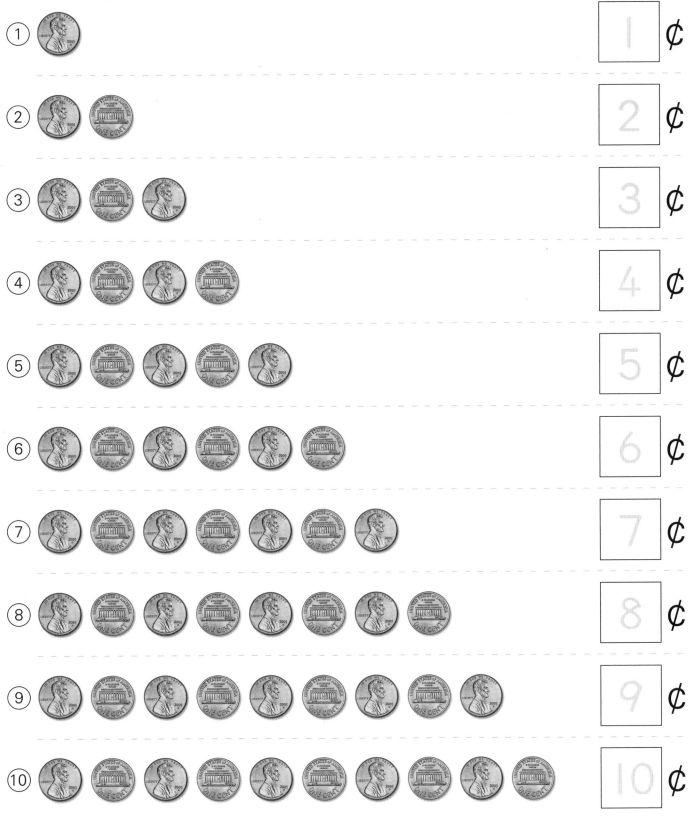

Name
Date

■ Add the value of each row of coins. Then trace the amount in the box on the right.

① 1 ¢

② 2 ¢

③ 3 ¢

④ 4 ¢

⑤ 5 ¢

⑥ 6 ¢

⑦ 7 ¢

⑧ 8 ¢

⑨ 9 ¢

⑩ 10 ¢

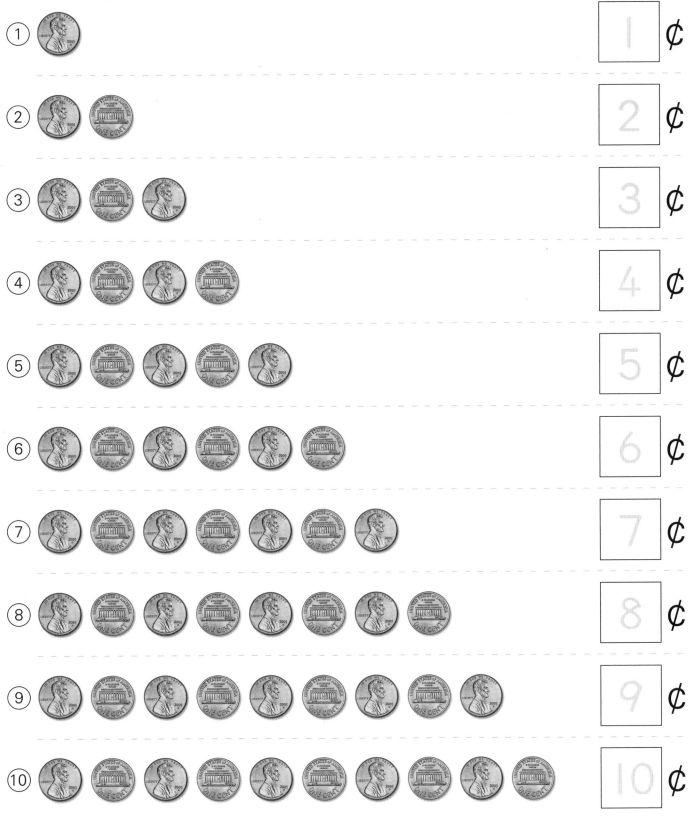

7

■Add the value of each row of coins. Then write the amount in the box on the right.

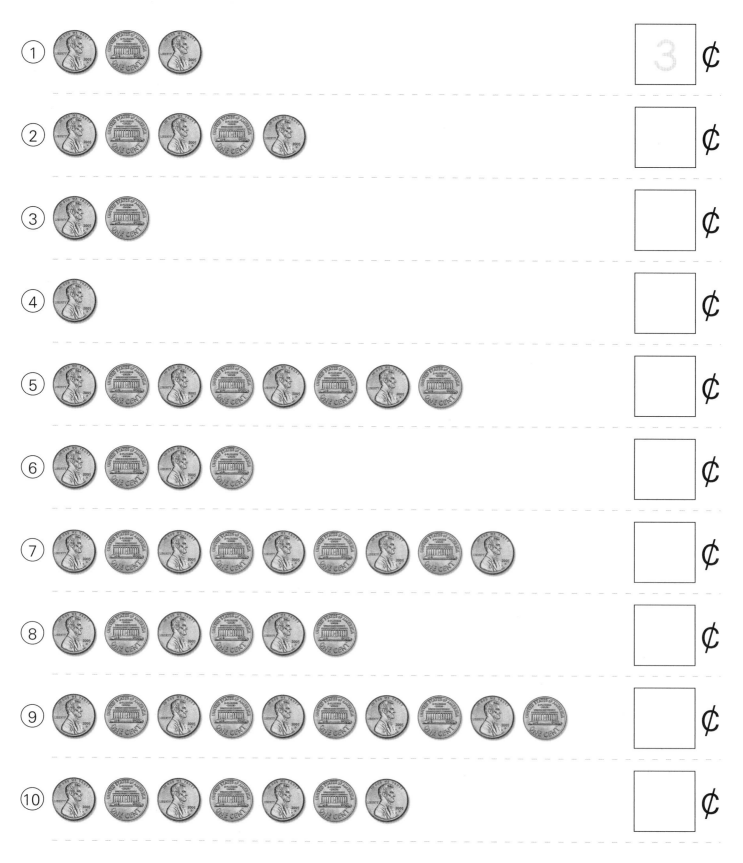

1   3 ¢

2   ☐ ¢

3   ☐ ¢

4   ☐ ¢

5   ☐ ¢

6   ☐ ¢

7   ☐ ¢

8   ☐ ¢

9   ☐ ¢

10   ☐ ¢

5 Counting Coins
11¢ to 15¢

Name

Date

■ Add the value of each group of coins. Then trace the amount in the box on the right.

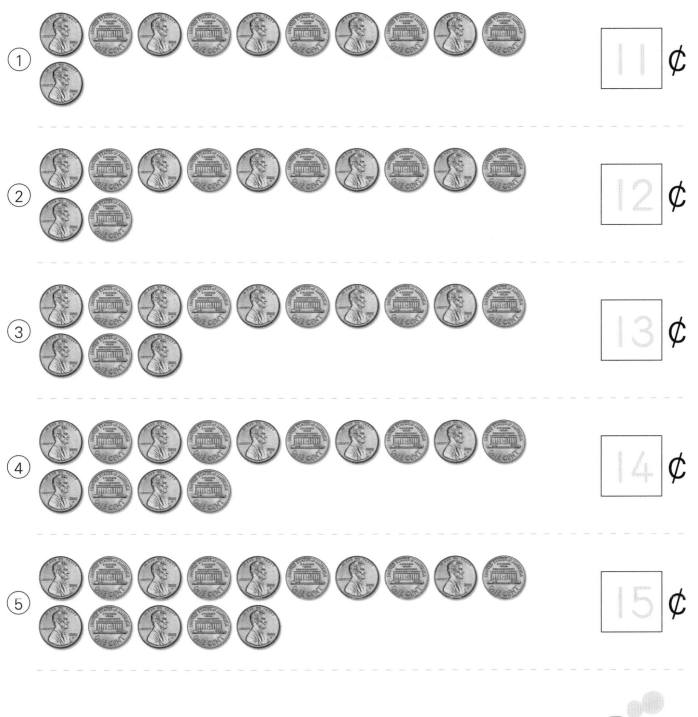

① 11 ¢

② 12 ¢

③ 13 ¢

④ 14 ¢

⑤ 15 ¢

■Add the value of each group of coins. Then write the amount in the box on the right.

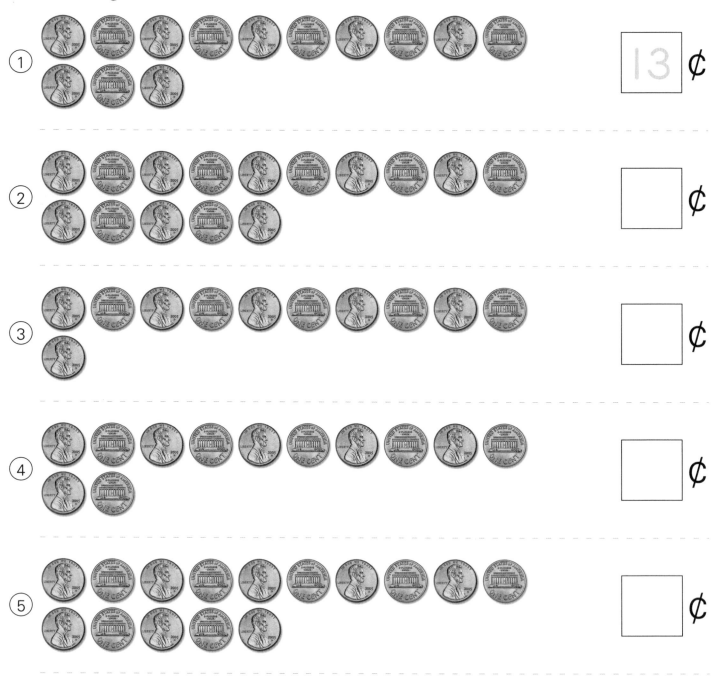

① 13 ¢

② ¢

③ ¢

④ ¢

⑤ ¢

6 Counting Coins
16¢ to 20¢

Name

Date

■ Add the value of each group of coins. Then trace the amount in the box on the right.

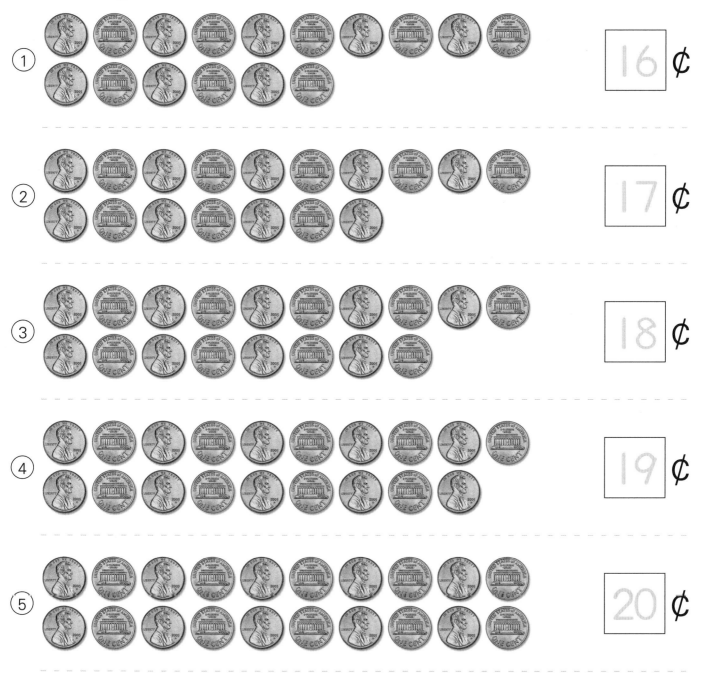

① [16] ¢

② [17] ¢

③ [18] ¢

④ [19] ¢

⑤ [20] ¢

11

Add the value of each group of coins. Then write the amount in the box on the right.

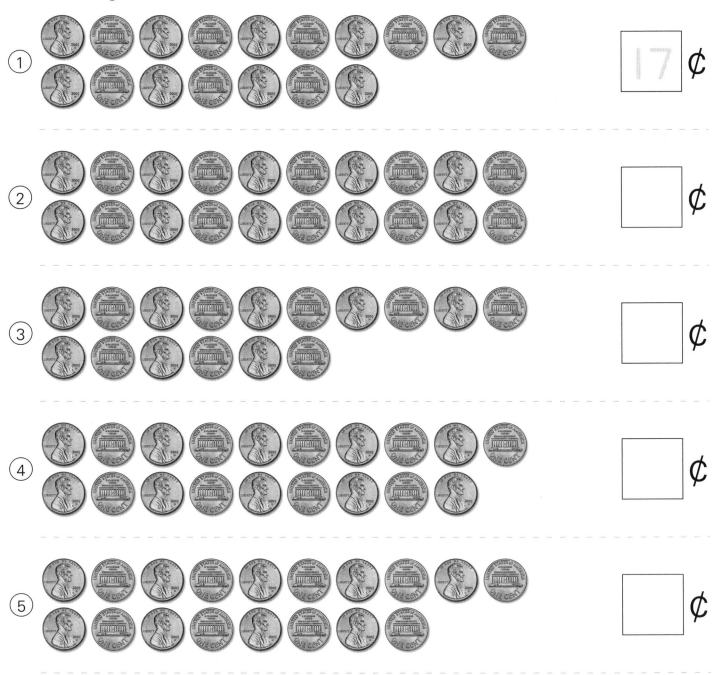

1. `17` ¢

2. ☐ ¢

3. ☐ ¢

4. ☐ ¢

5. ☐ ¢

Practicing Numbers
1 to 100

To parents In order to prepare for counting nickels, your child will practice tracing the multiples of five on this page. Once your child has finished tracing the numbers on the page, read the numbers he or she has traced aloud together. This is an important precursor to multiplication.

■ Say each number aloud while tracing it.

1	2	3	4	5	6	7	8	9	10
11	12	13	14	15	16	17	18	19	20
21	22	23	24	25	26	27	28	29	30
31	32	33	34	35	36	37	38	39	40
41	42	43	44	45	46	47	48	49	50
51	52	53	54	55	56	57	58	59	60
61	62	63	64	65	66	67	68	69	70
71	72	73	74	75	76	77	78	79	80
81	82	83	84	85	86	87	88	89	90
91	92	93	94	95	96	97	98	99	100

13

■ Say each number aloud while writing it.

1	2	3	4	5	6	7	8	9	
11	12	13	14		16	17	18	19	
21	22	23	24		26	27	28	29	
31	32	33	34		36	37	38	39	
41	42	43	44		46	47	48	49	
51	52	53	54		56	57	58	59	
61	62	63	64		66	67	68	69	
71	72	73	74		76	77	78	79	
81	82	83	84		86	87	88	89	
91	92	93	94		96	97	98	99	

5	10	15	20	25	30	35	40	45	50
5									50
55	60	65	70	75	80	85	90	95	100
									100

14

| Name |
| Date |

To parents On this page, your child will begin counting coins that are worth more than one cent. If your child encounters difficulty, try using pocket change to help your child understand that five pennies equal a nickel.

Front

5¢

nickel

Back

5¢

■ Add the value of each row of coins. Then trace the amount in the box on the right.

① 5 ¢   1 nickel

② 5 ¢   1 nickel

③ 10 ¢   2 nickels

④ 10 ¢   2 nickels

⑤ 10 ¢   2 nickels

■ Add the value of each row of coins. Then trace the amount in the box on the right.

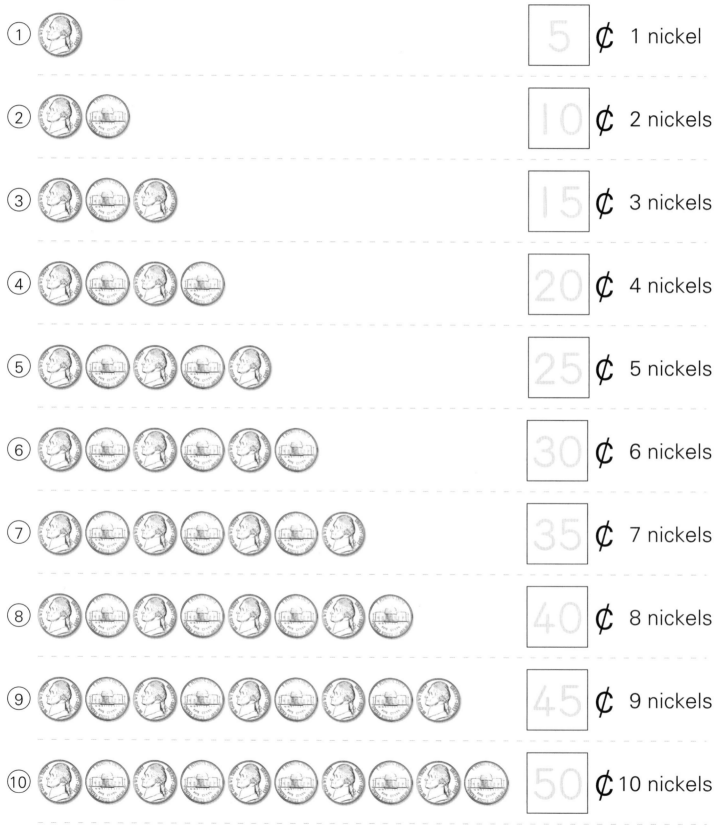

1. 5 ¢ 1 nickel

2. 10 ¢ 2 nickels

3. 15 ¢ 3 nickels

4. 20 ¢ 4 nickels

5. 25 ¢ 5 nickels

6. 30 ¢ 6 nickels

7. 35 ¢ 7 nickels

8. 40 ¢ 8 nickels

9. 45 ¢ 9 nickels

10. 50 ¢ 10 nickels

9 Counting Coins
5¢ to 50¢

Name

Date

■ Add the value of each row of coins. Then trace the amount in the box on the right.

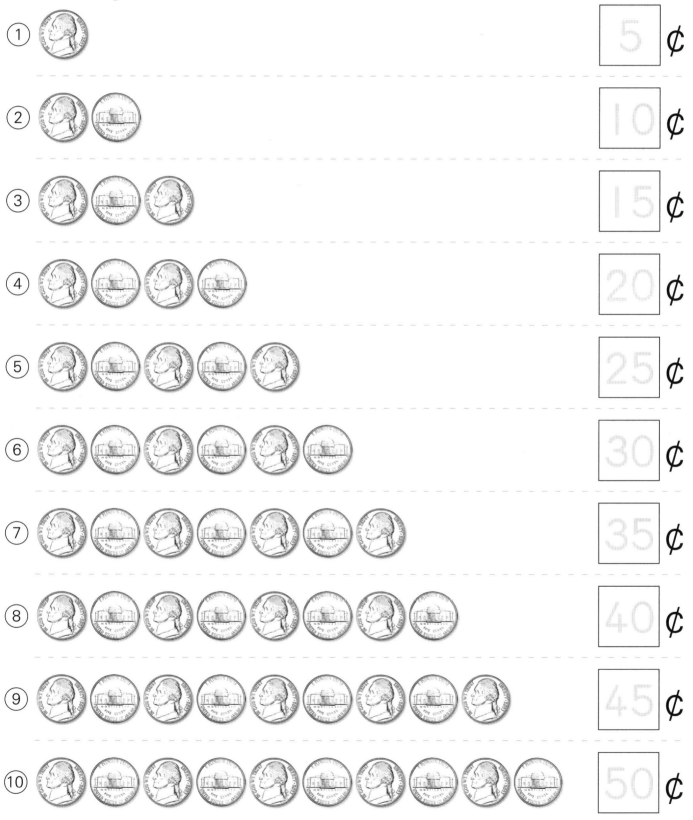

1. 5 ¢

2. 10 ¢

3. 15 ¢

4. 20 ¢

5. 25 ¢

6. 30 ¢

7. 35 ¢

8. 40 ¢

9. 45 ¢

10. 50 ¢

■ Add the value of each row of coins. Then write the amount in the box on the right.

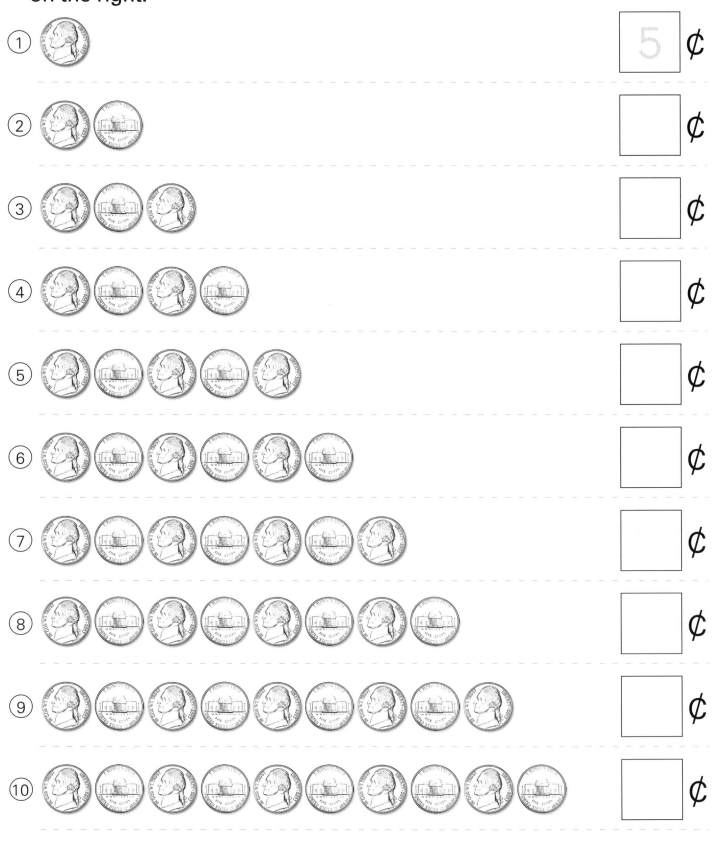

1. 5 ¢
2. ¢
3. ¢
4. ¢
5. ¢
6. ¢
7. ¢
8. ¢
9. ¢
10. ¢

10 Counting Coins
5¢ to 50¢

Name

Date

■ Add the value of each row of coins. Then write the amount in the box on the right.

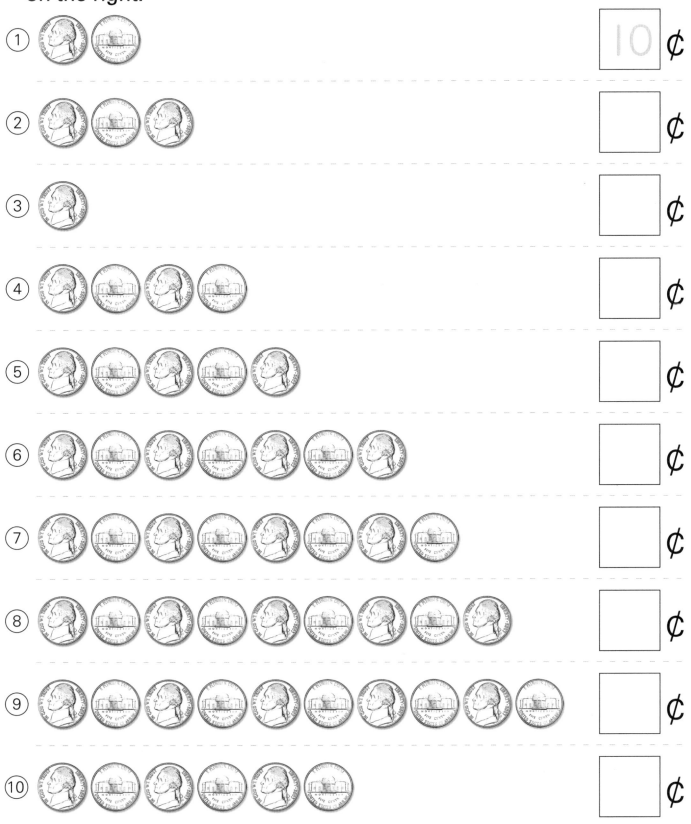

① ... 10 ¢

② ... ¢

③ ... ¢

④ ... ¢

⑤ ... ¢

⑥ ... ¢

⑦ ... ¢

⑧ ... ¢

⑨ ... ¢

⑩ ... ¢

■ Add the value of each row of coins. Then write the amount in the box on the right.

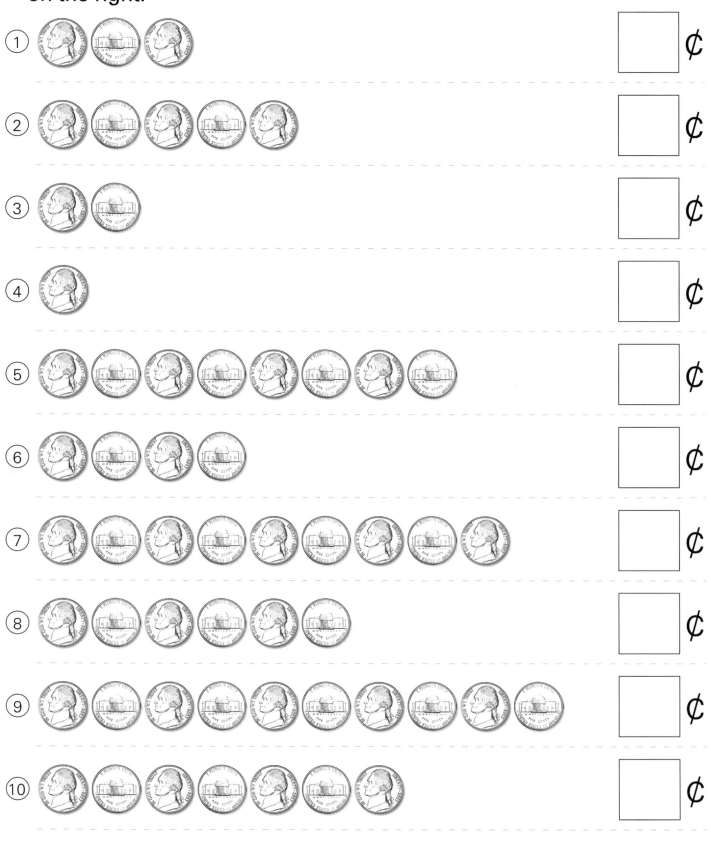

1. ☐ ¢

2. ☐ ¢

3. ☐ ¢

4. ☐ ¢

5. ☐ ¢

6. ☐ ¢

7. ☐ ¢

8. ☐ ¢

9. ☐ ¢

10. ☐ ¢

11 Review
Pennies and Nickels

■ Add the value of each row of coins. Then write the amount in the box on the right.

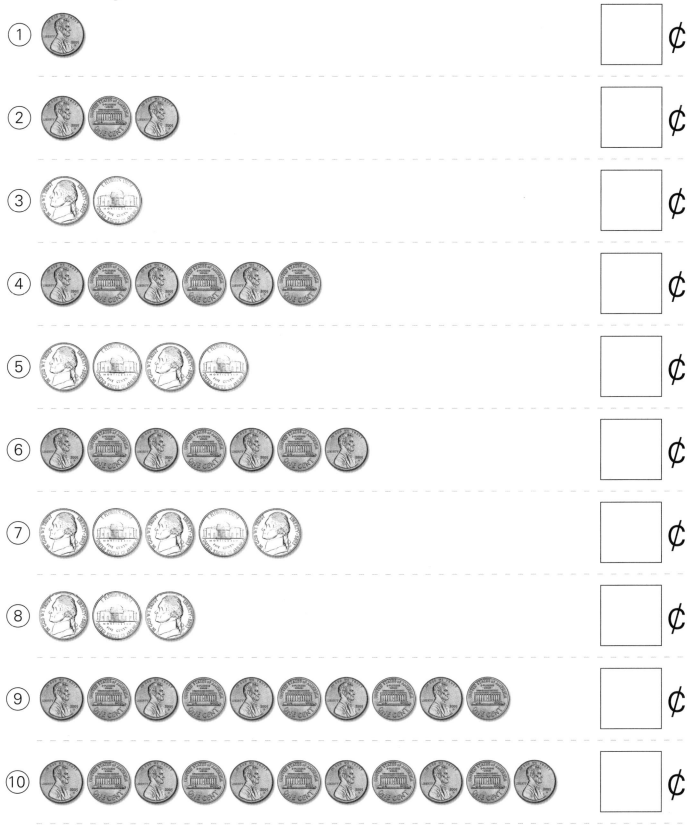

1

2

3

4

5

6

7

8

9

10

¢

¢

¢

¢

¢

¢

¢

¢

¢

¢

21

■ Add the value of each group of coins. Then write the amount in the box on the right.

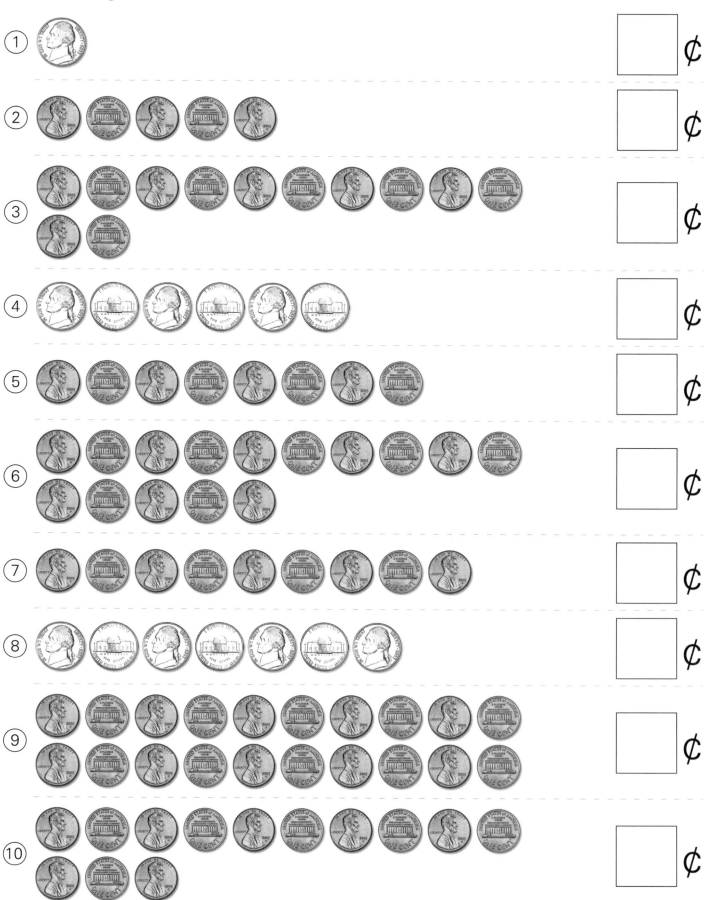

1. ⬜ ¢

2. ⬜ ¢

3. ⬜ ¢

4. ⬜ ¢

5. ⬜ ¢

6. ⬜ ¢

7. ⬜ ¢

8. ⬜ ¢

9. ⬜ ¢

10. ⬜ ¢

12 Practicing Numbers
1 to 100

Name

Date

■ Say each number aloud while tracing it.

1	2	3	4	5	6	7	8	9	10
11	12	13	14	15	16	17	18	19	20
21	22	23	24	25	26	27	28	29	30
31	32	33	34	35	36	37	38	39	40
41	42	43	44	45	46	47	48	49	50
51	52	53	54	55	56	57	58	59	60
61	62	63	64	65	66	67	68	69	70
71	72	73	74	75	76	77	78	79	80
81	82	83	84	85	86	87	88	89	90
91	92	93	94	95	96	97	98	99	100

■Say each number aloud while writing it.

1	2	3	4	5	6	7	8	9	10
11	12	13	14	15	16	17	18	19	
21	22	23	24	25	26	27	28	29	
31	32	33	34	35	36	37	38	39	
41	42	43	44	45	46	47	48	49	
51	52	53	54	55	56	57	58	59	
61	62	63	64	65	66	67	68	69	
71	72	73	74	75	76	77	78	79	
81	82	83	84	85	86	87	88	89	
91	92	93	94	95	96	97	98	99	

10	20	30	40	50	60	70	80	90	100
10									

24

13 Introducing Coins
The Dime

To parents Understanding that one coin is worth ten of another is very difficult. Help your child by counting out ten plus ten aloud. Offer lots of praise when your child understands this concept.

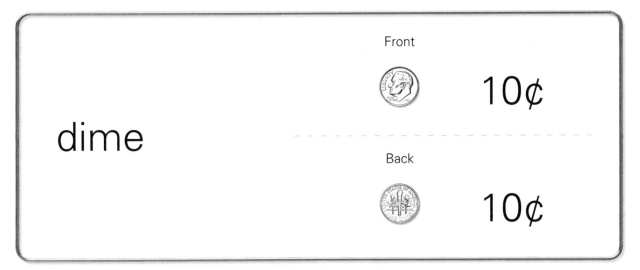

dime

Front

10¢

Back

10¢

■ Add the value of each row of coins. Then trace the amount in the box on the right.

①   10 ¢   1 dime

②   10 ¢   1 dime

③   20 ¢   2 dimes

④   20 ¢   2 dimes

⑤   20 ¢   2 dimes

■ Add the value of each row of coins. Then trace the amount in the box on the right.

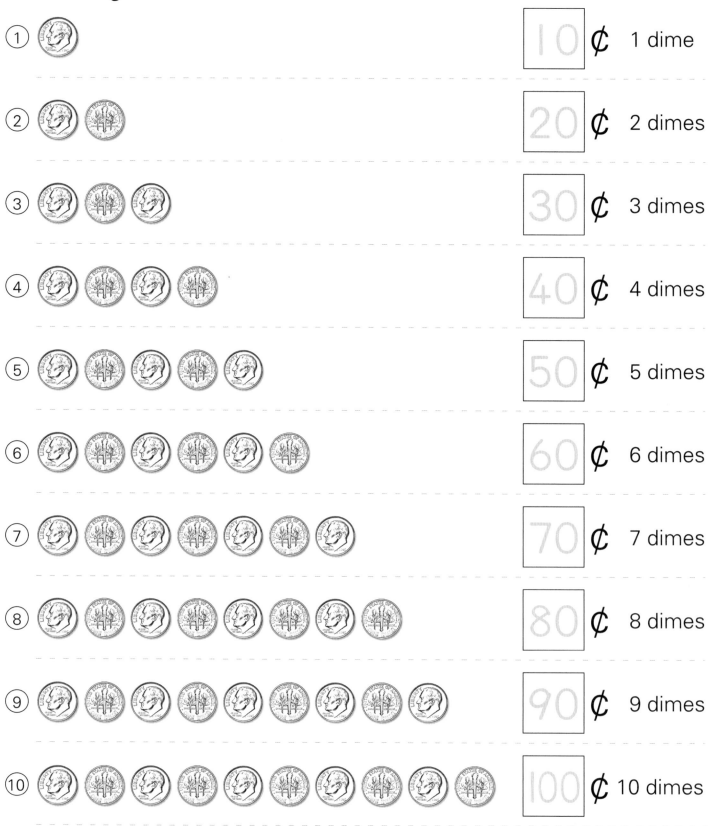

1. 10 ¢ 1 dime

2. 20 ¢ 2 dimes

3. 30 ¢ 3 dimes

4. 40 ¢ 4 dimes

5. 50 ¢ 5 dimes

6. 60 ¢ 6 dimes

7. 70 ¢ 7 dimes

8. 80 ¢ 8 dimes

9. 90 ¢ 9 dimes

10. 100 ¢ 10 dimes

Counting Coins
10¢ to 100¢

■ Add the value of each row of coins. Then trace the amount in the box on the right.

①   10 ¢

②   20 ¢

③   30 ¢

④   40 ¢

⑤   50 ¢

⑥   60 ¢

⑦   70 ¢

⑧   80 ¢

⑨   90 ¢

⑩   100 ¢

■ Add the value of each row of coins. Then write the amount in the box on the right.

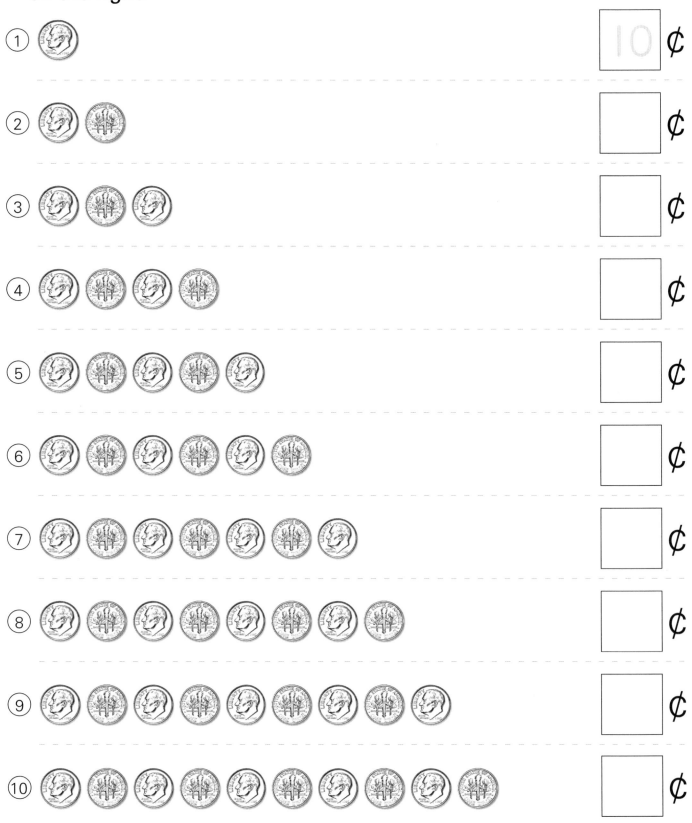

1. 10 ¢

2. ¢

3. ¢

4. ¢

5. ¢

6. ¢

7. ¢

8. ¢

9. ¢

10. ¢

15 Counting Coins
10¢ to 100¢

Name

Date

■ Add the value of each row of coins. Then write the amount in the box on the right.

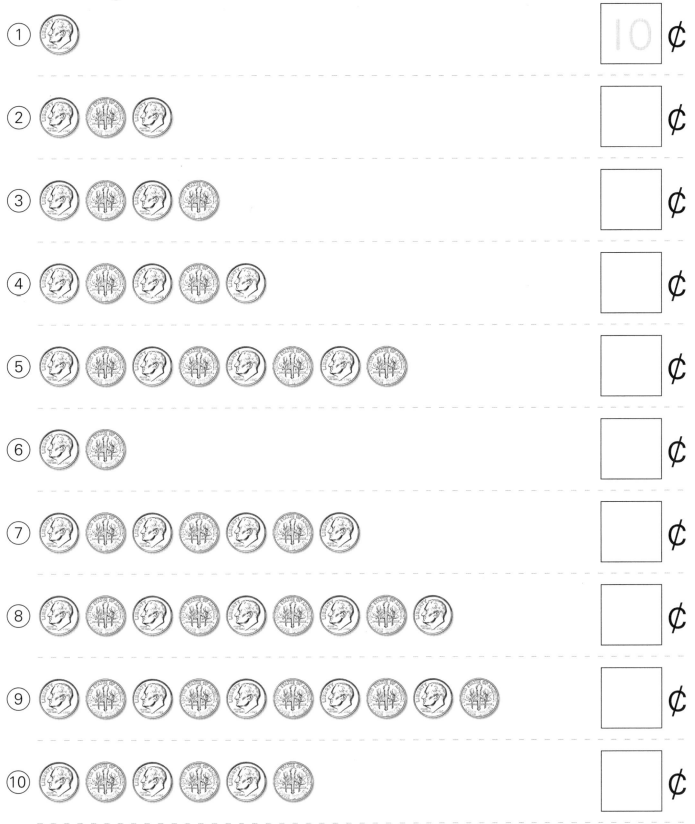

1. $\boxed{10}$ ¢

2. $\boxed{}$ ¢

3. $\boxed{}$ ¢

4. $\boxed{}$ ¢

5. $\boxed{}$ ¢

6. $\boxed{}$ ¢

7. $\boxed{}$ ¢

8. $\boxed{}$ ¢

9. $\boxed{}$ ¢

10. $\boxed{}$ ¢

■ Add the value of each row of coins. Then write the amount in the box on the right.

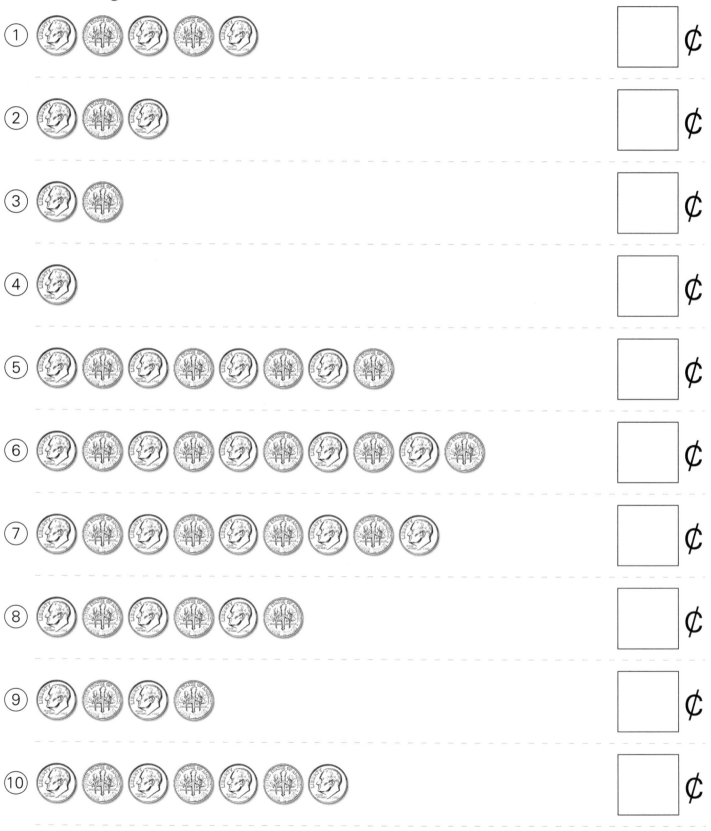

① _____ ¢

② _____ ¢

③ _____ ¢

④ _____ ¢

⑤ _____ ¢

⑥ _____ ¢

⑦ _____ ¢

⑧ _____ ¢

⑨ _____ ¢

⑩ _____ ¢

16 Practicing Numbers
1 to 100

Name

Date

■Say each number aloud while tracing it.

1	2	3	4	5	6	7	8	9	10
11	12	13	14	15	16	17	18	19	20
21	22	23	24	25	26	27	28	29	30
31	32	33	34	35	36	37	38	39	40
41	42	43	44	45	46	47	48	49	50
51	52	53	54	55	56	57	58	59	60
61	62	63	64	65	66	67	68	69	70
71	72	73	74	75	76	77	78	79	80
81	82	83	84	85	86	87	88	89	90
91	92	93	94	95	96	97	98	99	100

■Say each number aloud while writing it.

1	2	3	4	5	6	7	8	9	10
11	12	13	14	15	16	17	18	19	20
21	22	23	24	25	26	27	28	29	30
31	32	33	34	35	36	37	38	39	40
41	42	43	44	45	46	47	48	49	
51	52	53	54	55	56	57	58	59	60
61	62	63	64	65	66	67	68	69	70
71	72	73	74		76	77	78	79	80
81	82	83	84	85	86	87	88	89	90
91	92	93	94	95	96	97	98	99	

25	50	75	100
25			

Introducing Coins
The Quarter

Name

Date

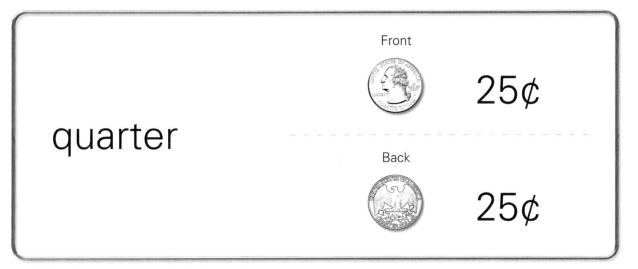

Front

25¢

quarter

Back

25¢

■ Add the value of each row of coins. Then trace the amount in the box on the right.

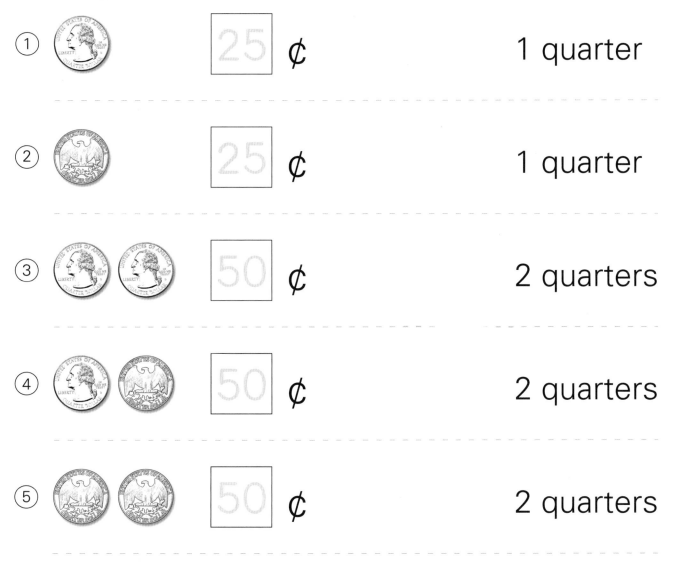

① 25 ¢   1 quarter

② 25 ¢   1 quarter

③ 50 ¢   2 quarters

④ 50 ¢   2 quarters

⑤ 50 ¢   2 quarters

■ Add the value of each row of coins. Then trace or write the amount
in the box on the right.

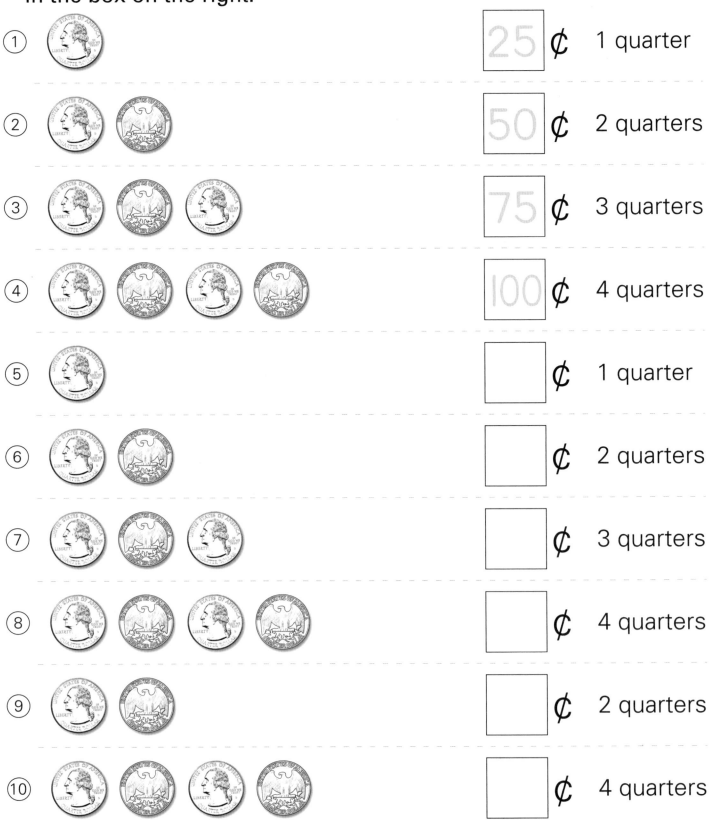

1. 25 ¢   1 quarter

2. 50 ¢   2 quarters

3. 75 ¢   3 quarters

4. 100 ¢   4 quarters

5. ☐ ¢   1 quarter

6. ☐ ¢   2 quarters

7. ☐ ¢   3 quarters

8. ☐ ¢   4 quarters

9. ☐ ¢   2 quarters

10. ☐ ¢   4 quarters

34

Counting Coins
25¢ to 100¢

Name

Date

■ Add the value of each row of coins. Then trace or write the amount in the box on the right.

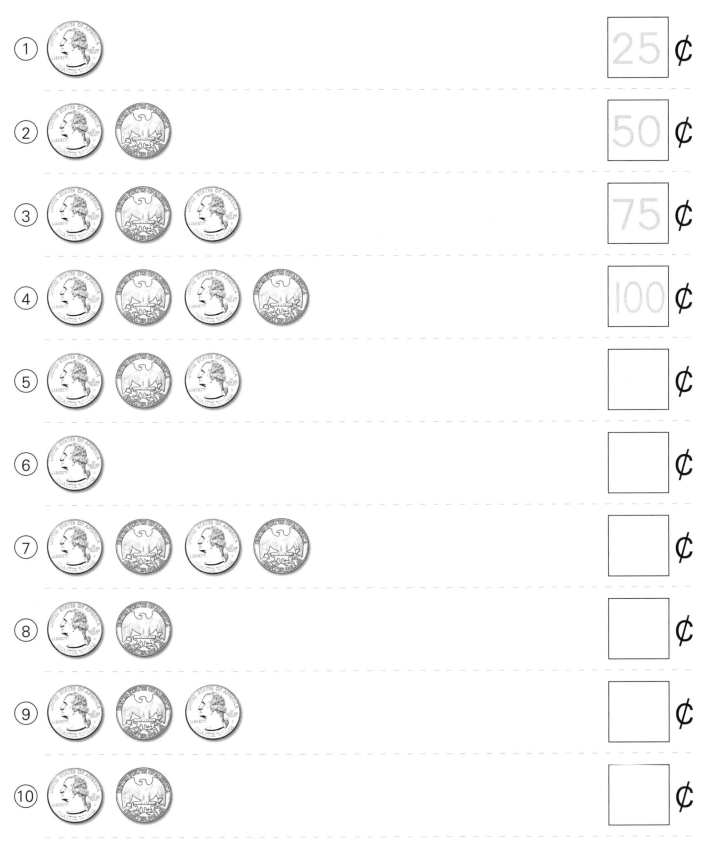

① 25 ¢

② 50 ¢

③ 75 ¢

④ 100 ¢

⑤ ☐ ¢

⑥ ☐ ¢

⑦ ☐ ¢

⑧ ☐ ¢

⑨ ☐ ¢

⑩ ☐ ¢

■ Add the value of each row of coins. Then write the amount in the box on the right.

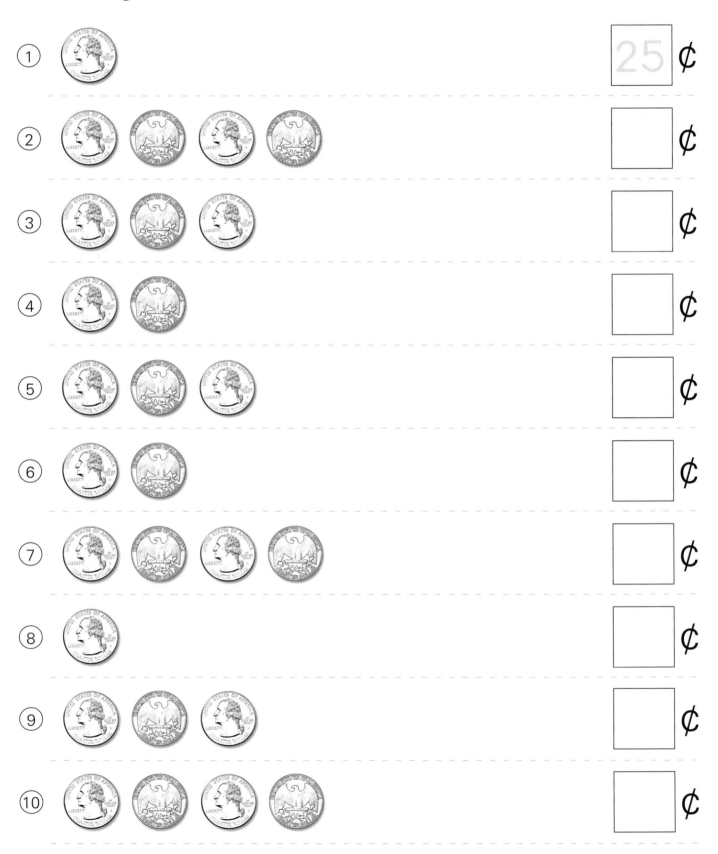

1. 25 ¢

2. ☐ ¢

3. ☐ ¢

4. ☐ ¢

5. ☐ ¢

6. ☐ ¢

7. ☐ ¢

8. ☐ ¢

9. ☐ ¢

10. ☐ ¢

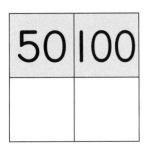

19 Practicing Numbers
1 to 100

■ Say each number aloud while writing it.

1	2	3	4	5	6	7	8	9	10
11	12	13	14	15	16	17	18	19	20
21	22	23	24	25	26	27	28	29	30
31	32	33	34	35	36	37	38	39	40
41	42	43	44	45	46	47	48	49	50
51	52	53	54	55	56	57	58	59	60
61	62	63	64	65	66	67	68	69	70
71	72	73	74	75	76	77	78	79	80
81	82	83	84	85	86	87	88	89	90
91	92	93	94	95	96	97	98	99	

50	100

37

Introducing Coins
The Half Dollar

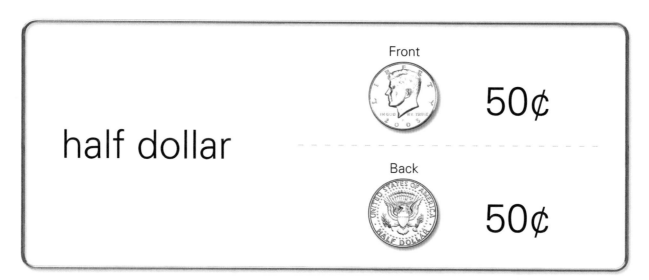

half dollar

Front 50¢

Back 50¢

■ Add the value of each row of coins. Then trace the amount in the box on the right.

1. 50 ¢   1 half dollar

2. 50 ¢   1 half dollar

3. 100 ¢   2 half dollars

4. 100 ¢   2 half dollars

5. 100 ¢   2 half dollars

Review
All coins

Name

Date

■ Add the value of each row of coins. Then write the amount in the box on the right.

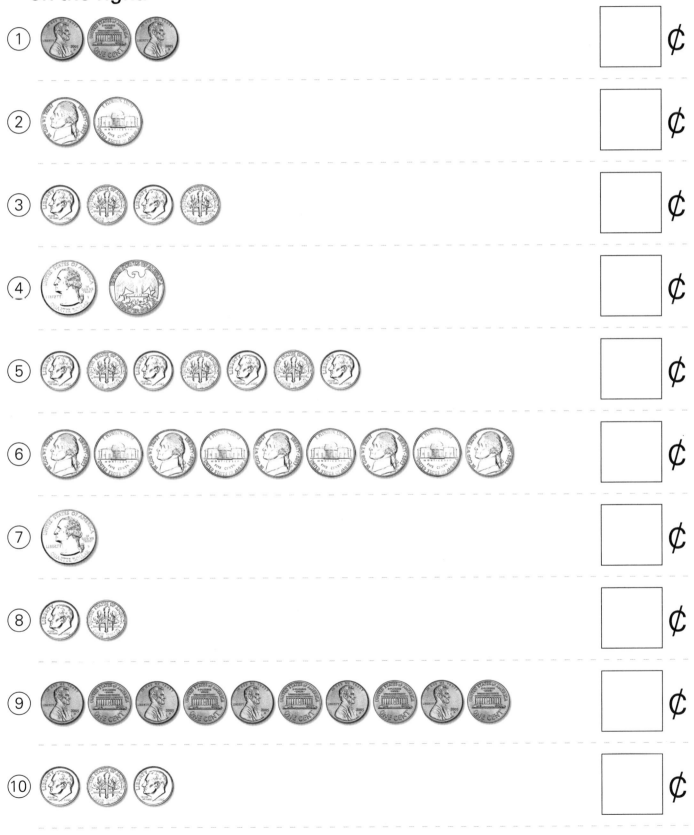

① ☐ ¢

② ☐ ¢

③ ☐ ¢

④ ☐ ¢

⑤ ☐ ¢

⑥ ☐ ¢

⑦ ☐ ¢

⑧ ☐ ¢

⑨ ☐ ¢

⑩ ☐ ¢

■ Add the value of each group of coins. Then write the amount in the box on the right.

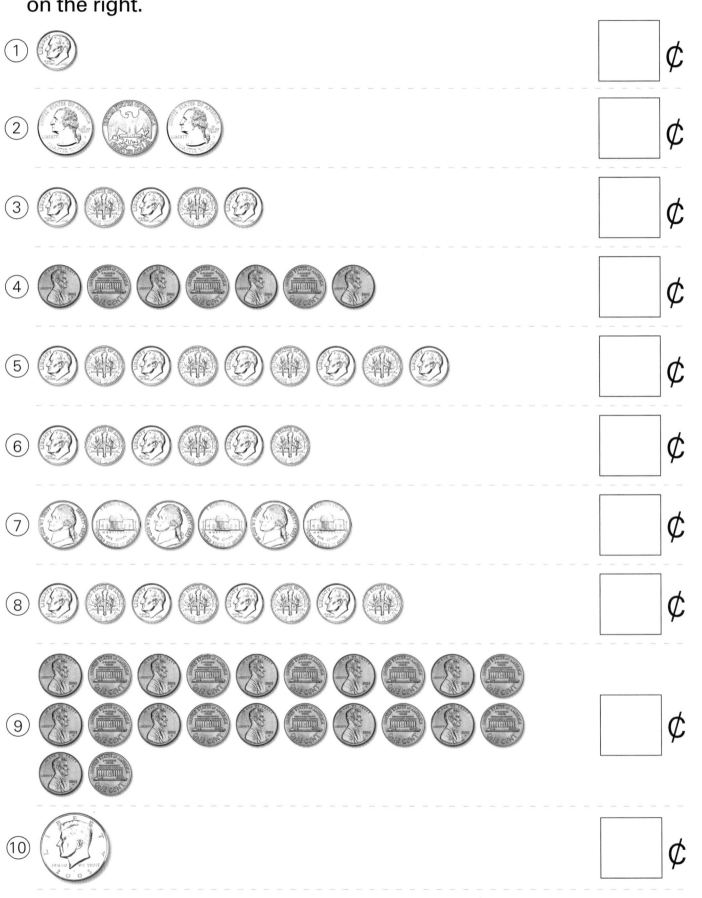

1   ☐ ¢

2   ☐ ¢

3   ☐ ¢

4   ☐ ¢

5   ☐ ¢

6   ☐ ¢

7   ☐ ¢

8   ☐ ¢

9   ☐ ¢

10   ☐ ¢

Name

Date

■ Add the value of the coins in each purse. Then write the amount in the box on the right.

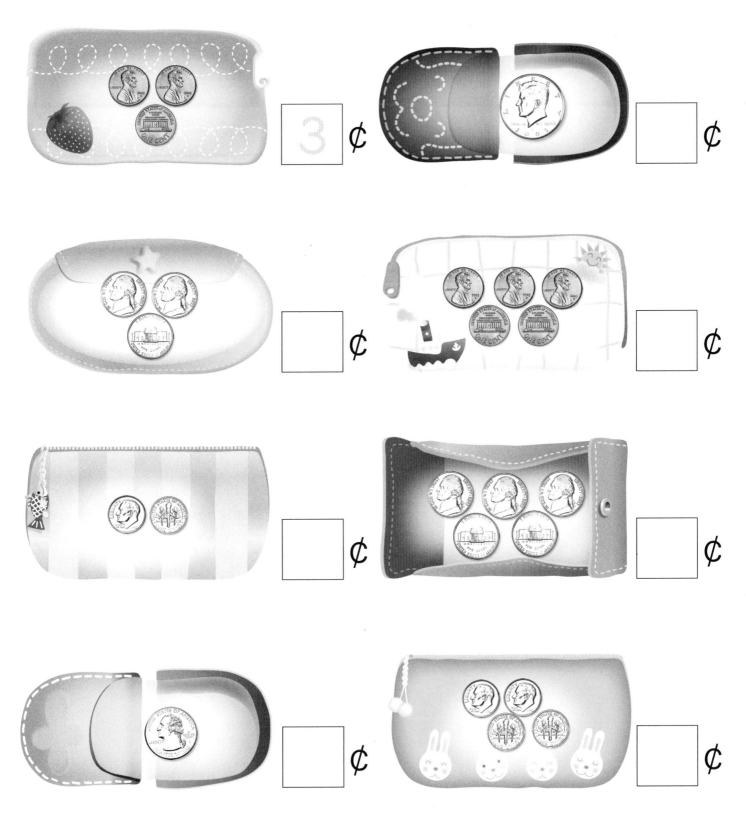

■Add the value of the coins in each purse. Then write the amount in the box on the right.

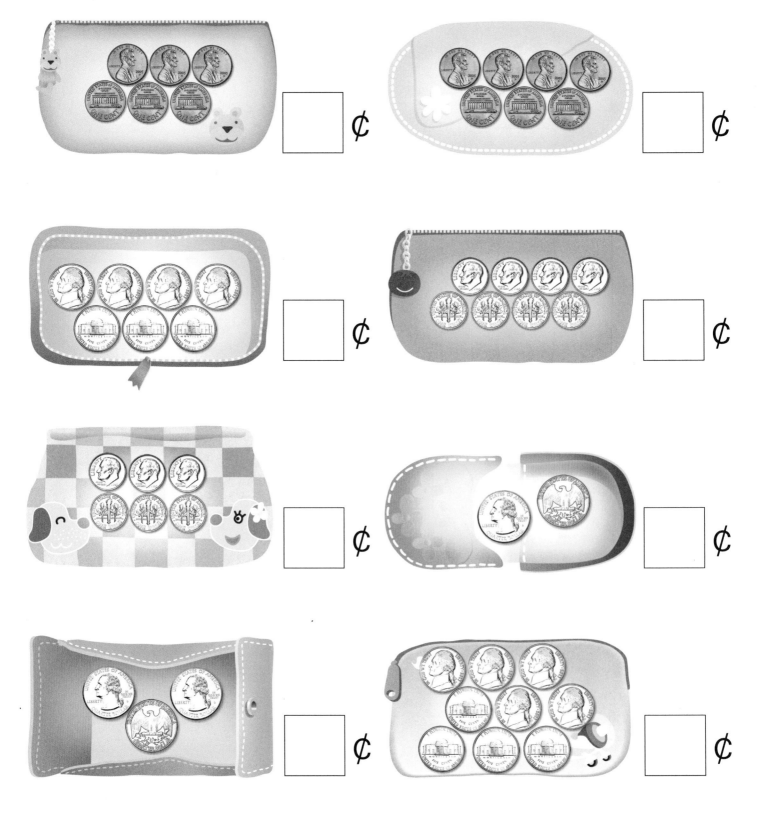

42

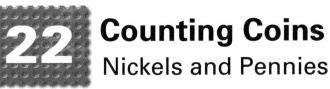

Counting Coins
Nickels and Pennies

To parents Now that your child understands the relative value of each coin, he or she will practice adding them together. Having real change on hand will help your child with these exercises.

■ Add the value of each row of coins. Then trace the amount in the box on the right.

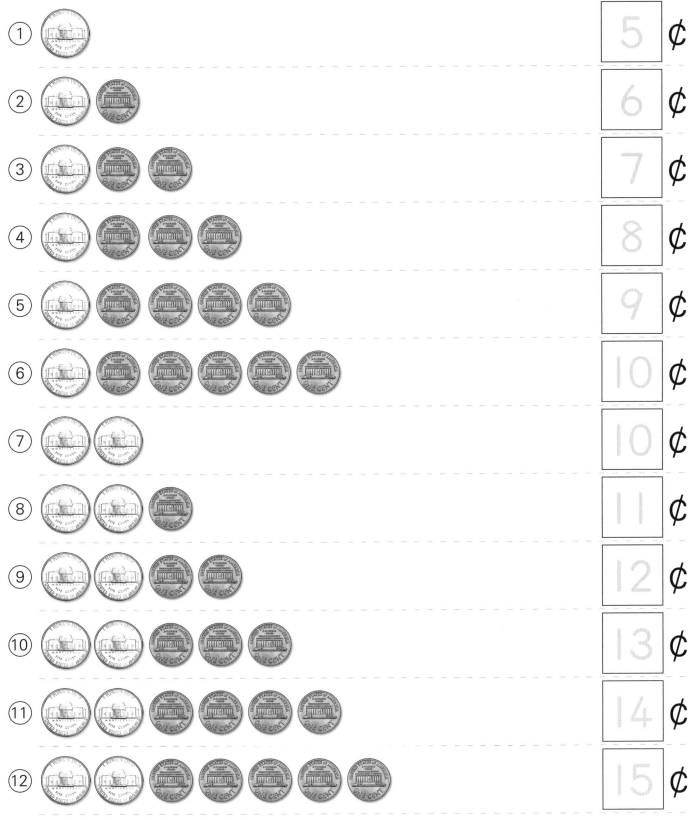

43

■ Add the value of each row of coins. Then write the amount in the box on the right.

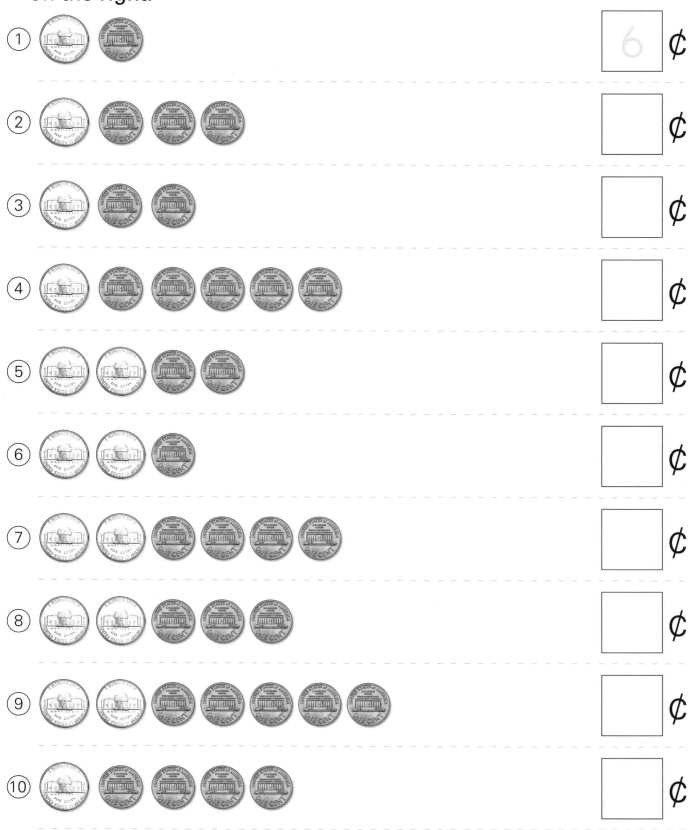

1. 6 ¢
2. ☐ ¢
3. ☐ ¢
4. ☐ ¢
5. ☐ ¢
6. ☐ ¢
7. ☐ ¢
8. ☐ ¢
9. ☐ ¢
10. ☐ ¢

23 Counting Coins
Nickels and Pennies

■ Add the value of each row of coins. Then trace the amount in the box on the right.

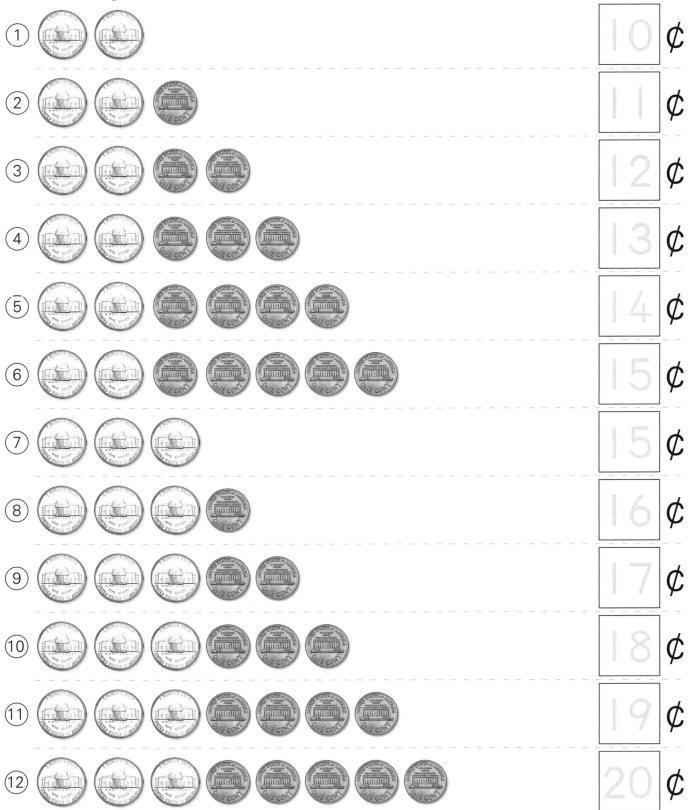

1. 10 ¢
2. 11 ¢
3. 12 ¢
4. 13 ¢
5. 14 ¢
6. 15 ¢
7. 15 ¢
8. 16 ¢
9. 17 ¢
10. 18 ¢
11. 19 ¢
12. 20 ¢

■ Add the value of each row of coins. Then write the amount in the box on the right.

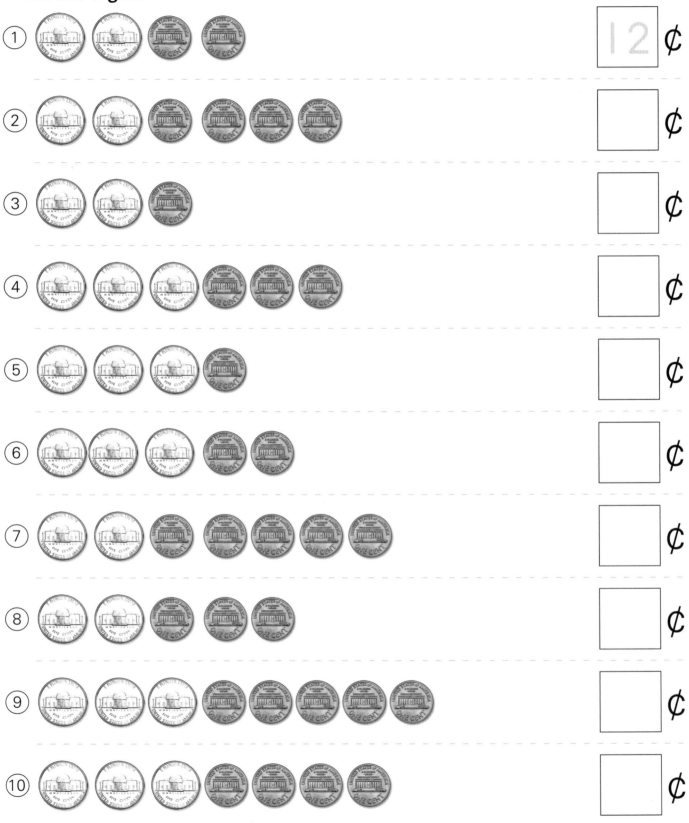

1) 12 ¢

2) ☐ ¢

3) ☐ ¢

4) ☐ ¢

5) ☐ ¢

6) ☐ ¢

7) ☐ ¢

8) ☐ ¢

9) ☐ ¢

10) ☐ ¢

Counting Coins
Dimes and Pennies

Name

Date

■ Add the value of each row of coins. Then trace the amount in the box on the right.

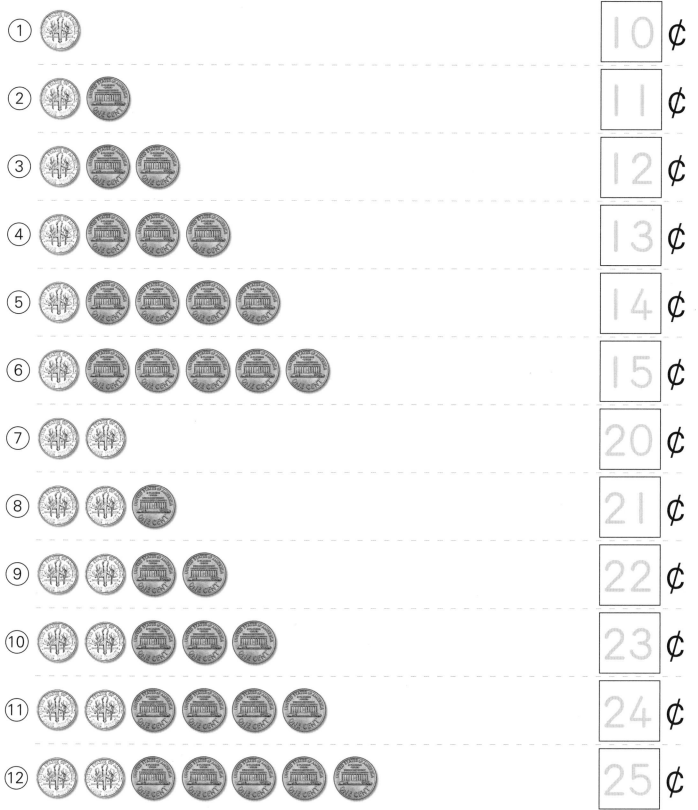

1. 10 ¢
2. 11 ¢
3. 12 ¢
4. 13 ¢
5. 14 ¢
6. 15 ¢
7. 20 ¢
8. 21 ¢
9. 22 ¢
10. 23 ¢
11. 24 ¢
12. 25 ¢

■ Add the value of each row of coins. Then write the amount in the box on the right.

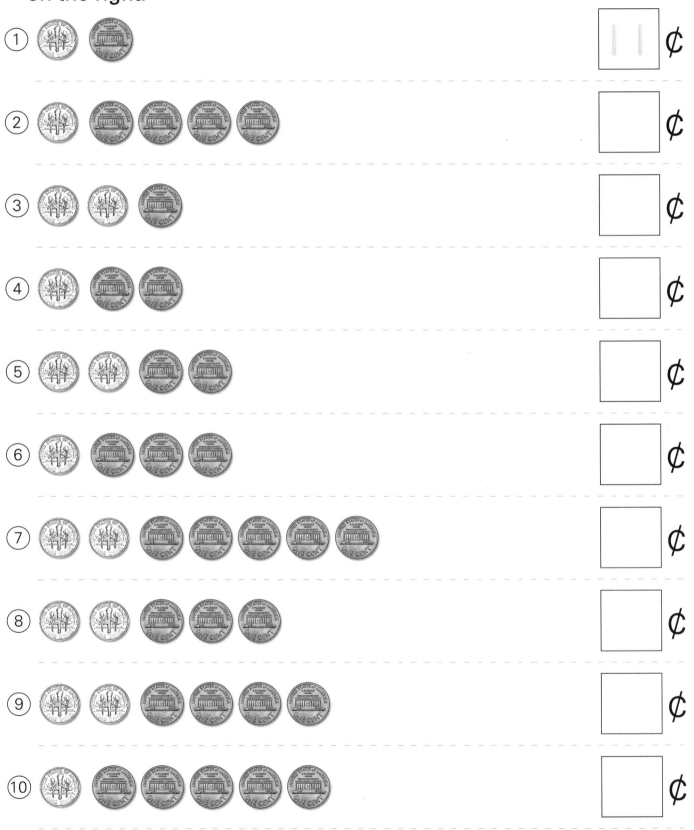

1. [dime] [penny]   ☐☐ ¢

2. [dime] [penny] [penny] [penny] [penny]   ☐ ¢

3. [dime] [dime] [penny]   ☐ ¢

4. [dime] [penny] [penny]   ☐ ¢

5. [dime] [dime] [penny] [penny]   ☐ ¢

6. [dime] [penny] [penny] [penny]   ☐ ¢

7. [dime] [dime] [penny] [penny] [penny] [penny] [penny]   ☐ ¢

8. [dime] [dime] [penny] [penny] [penny]   ☐ ¢

9. [dime] [dime] [penny] [penny] [penny] [penny]   ☐ ¢

10. [dime] [penny] [penny] [penny] [penny] [penny]   ☐ ¢

Counting Coins
Quarters and Pennies

Name	
Date	

■ Add the value of each row of coins. Then trace the amount in the box on the right.

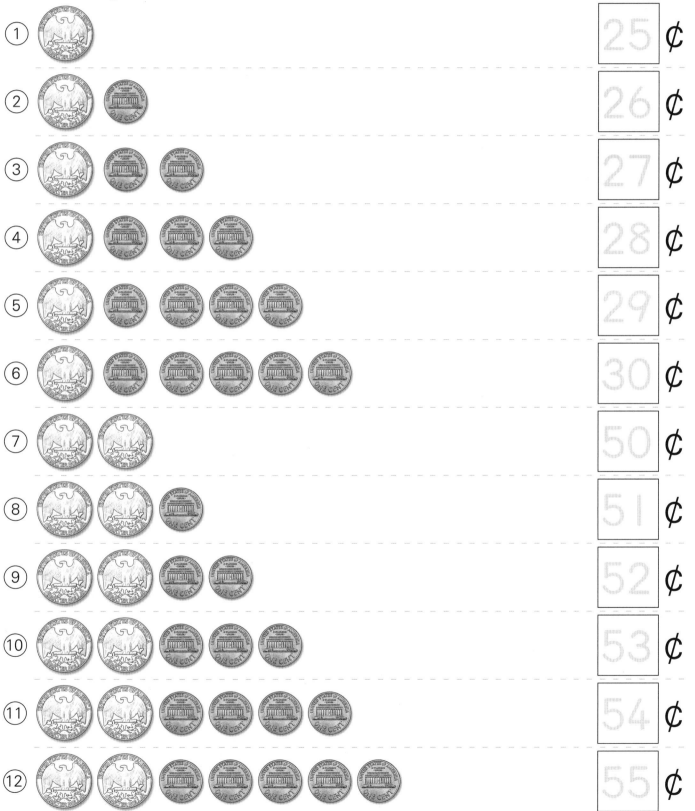

1. 25 ¢
2. 26 ¢
3. 27 ¢
4. 28 ¢
5. 29 ¢
6. 30 ¢
7. 50 ¢
8. 51 ¢
9. 52 ¢
10. 53 ¢
11. 54 ¢
12. 55 ¢

Add the value of each row of coins. Then write the amount in the box on the right.

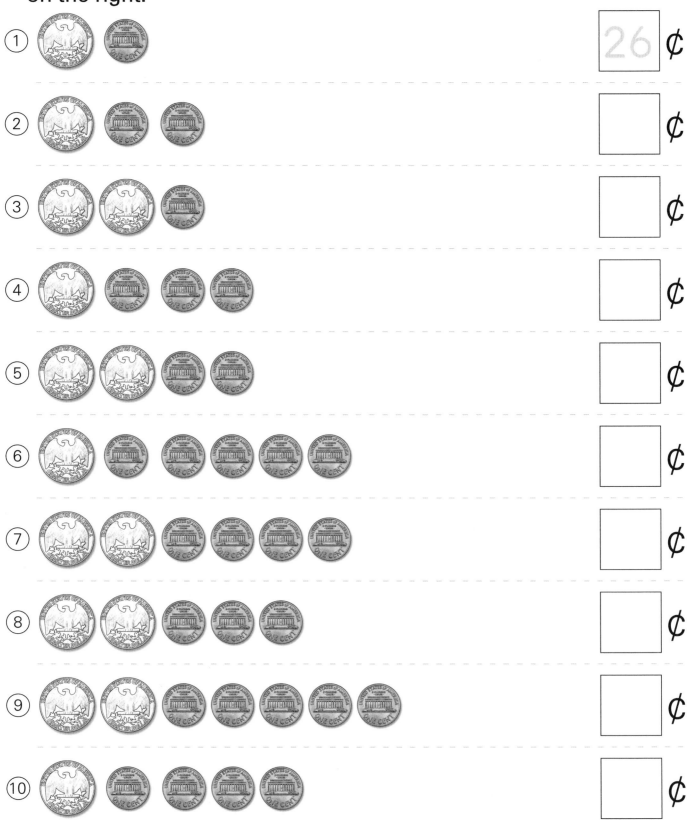

1. 26 ¢

2. ___ ¢

3. ___ ¢

4. ___ ¢

5. ___ ¢

6. ___ ¢

7. ___ ¢

8. ___ ¢

9. ___ ¢

10. ___ ¢

Counting Coins
Half Dollars and Pennies

Name

Date

■ Add the value of each row of coins. Then trace the amount in the box on the right.

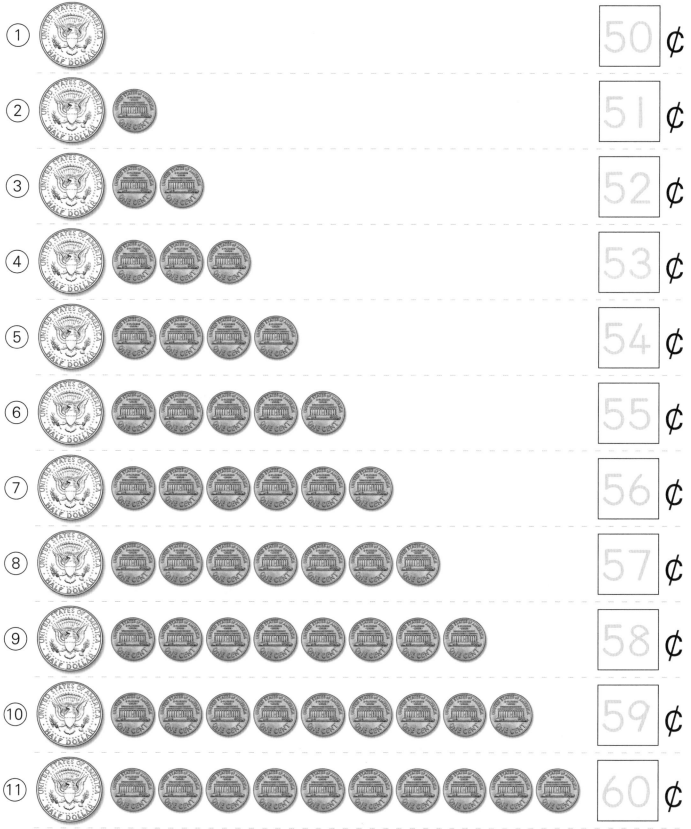

1. 50 ¢

2. 51 ¢

3. 52 ¢

4. 53 ¢

5. 54 ¢

6. 55 ¢

7. 56 ¢

8. 57 ¢

9. 58 ¢

10. 59 ¢

11. 60 ¢

■ Add the value of each row of coins. Then write the amount in the box on the right.

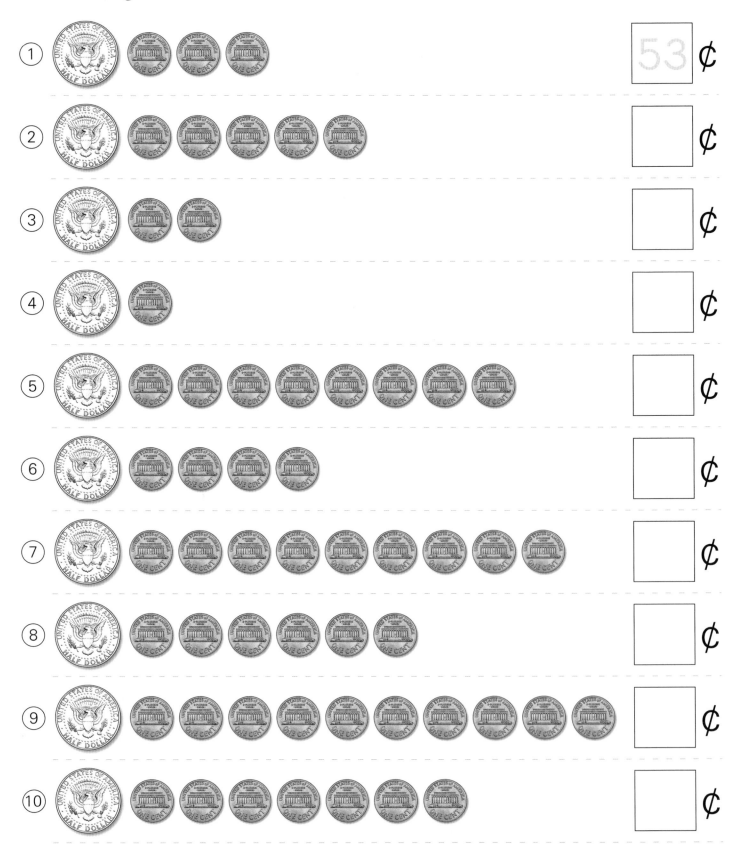

1. 53 ¢
2. ¢
3. ¢
4. ¢
5. ¢
6. ¢
7. ¢
8. ¢
9. ¢
10. ¢

52

27 Review
How Much?

Name

Date

To parents In this review, your child will add up the value of the coins in his or her piggy bank. You could start a piggy bank with your child in order to spark interest in this particular subject.

■ Add the value of the coins in each piggy bank. Then write the amount in the box on the right.

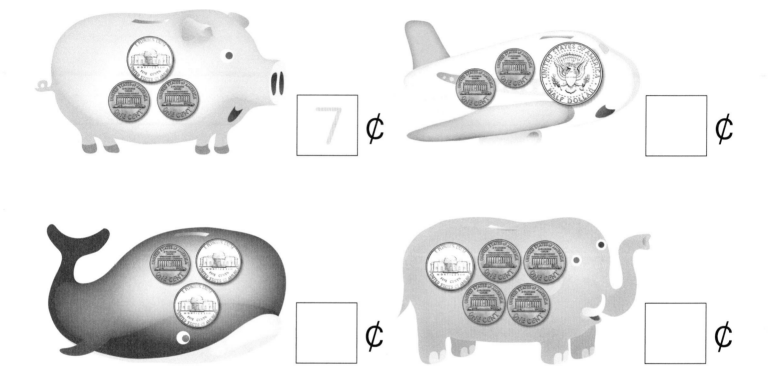

7 ¢

☐ ¢

☐ ¢

☐ ¢

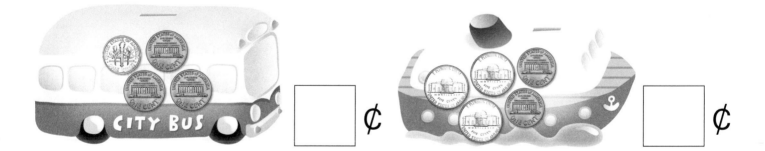

☐ ¢

☐ ¢

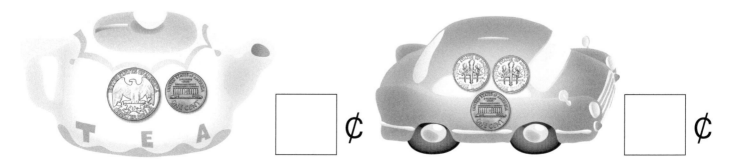

☐ ¢

☐ ¢

53

Add the value of the coins in each piggy bank. Then write the amount in the box on the right.

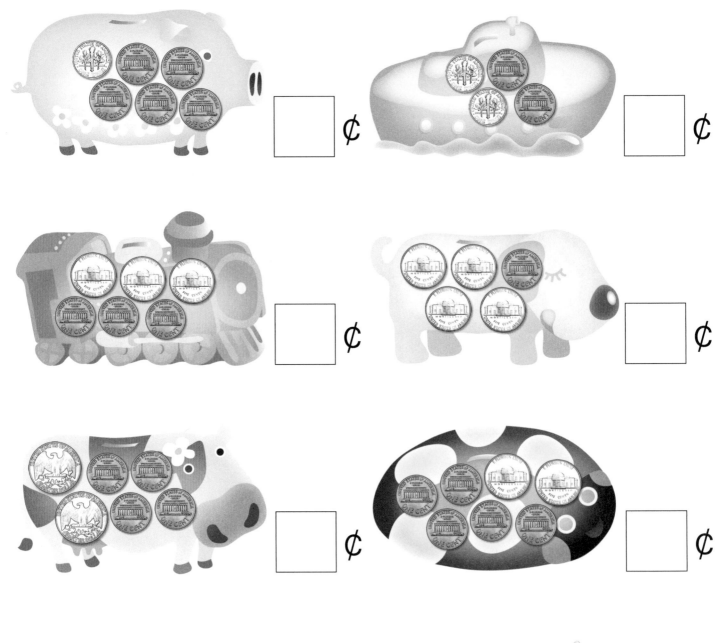

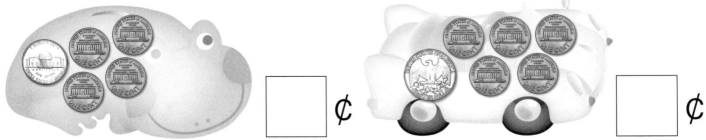

Counting Coins
Dimes and Nickels

■ Add the value of each row of coins. Then trace the amount in the box on the right.

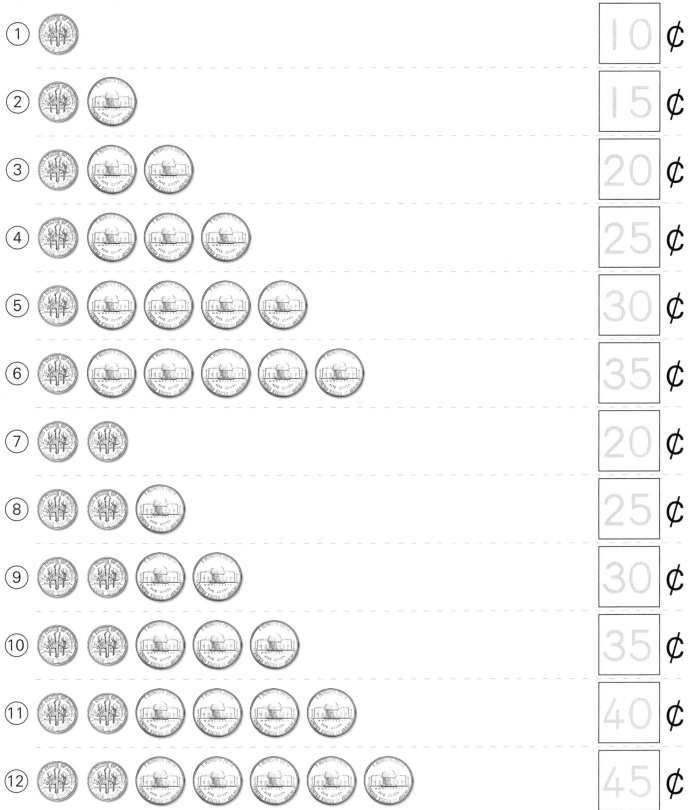

1. 10 ¢

2. 15 ¢

3. 20 ¢

4. 25 ¢

5. 30 ¢

6. 35 ¢

7. 20 ¢

8. 25 ¢

9. 30 ¢

10. 35 ¢

11. 40 ¢

12. 45 ¢

■ Add the value of each row of coins. Then write the amount in the box on the right.

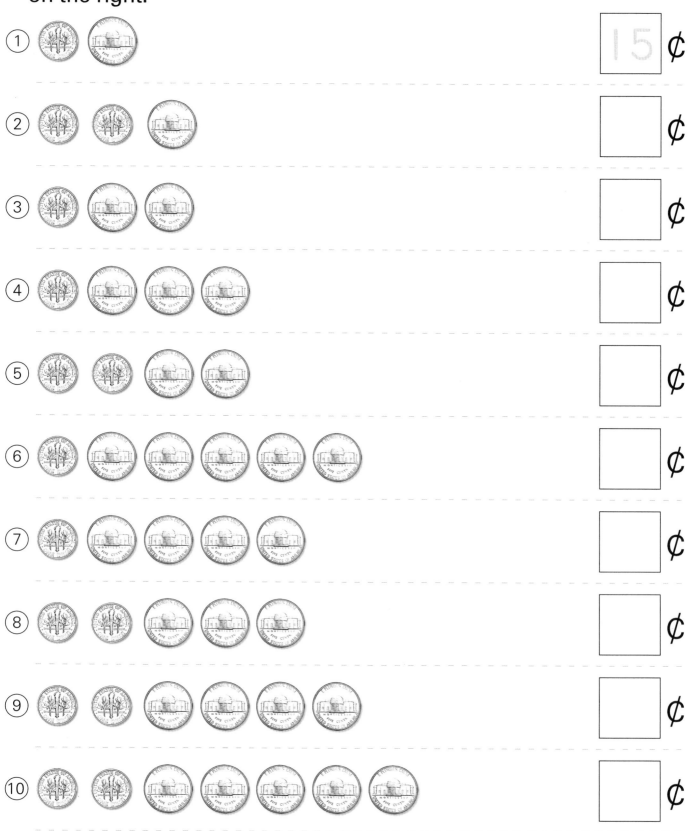

1. 15 ¢

2. ☐ ¢

3. ☐ ¢

4. ☐ ¢

5. ☐ ¢

6. ☐ ¢

7. ☐ ¢

8. ☐ ¢

9. ☐ ¢

10. ☐ ¢

Counting Coins
Quarters and Nickels

Name

Date

■ Add the value of each row of coins. Then trace the amount in the box on the right.

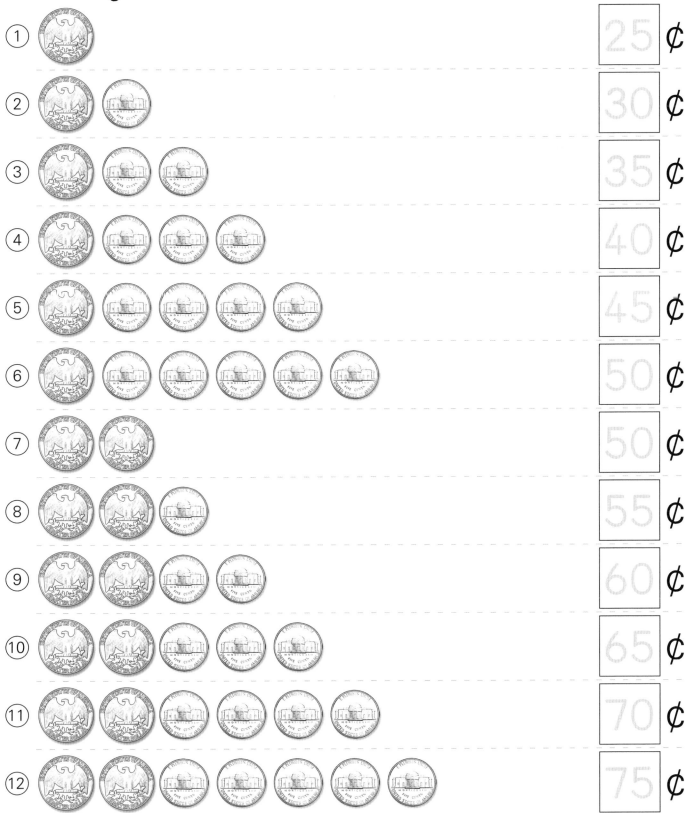

1. 25 ¢
2. 30 ¢
3. 35 ¢
4. 40 ¢
5. 45 ¢
6. 50 ¢
7. 50 ¢
8. 55 ¢
9. 60 ¢
10. 65 ¢
11. 70 ¢
12. 75 ¢

Add the value of each row of coins. Then write the amount in the box on the right.

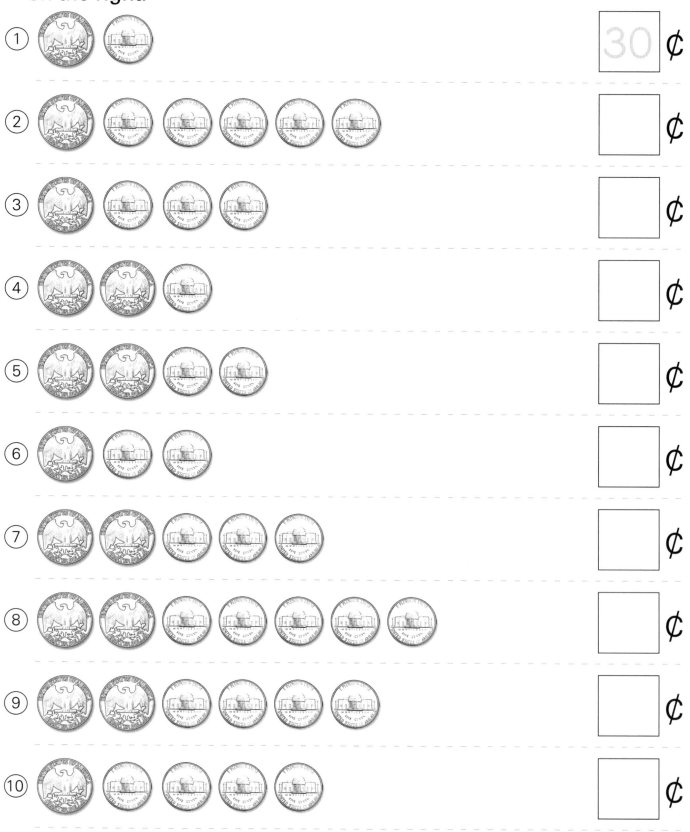

1. 30 ¢
2. ¢
3. ¢
4. ¢
5. ¢
6. ¢
7. ¢
8. ¢
9. ¢
10. ¢

30 Counting Coins
Dimes, Nickels and Pennies

To parents In this exercise, your child will have to add the values of three different coins together. You could help by asking what each coin is worth separately.

■ Add the value of each row of coins. Then trace the amount in the box on the right.

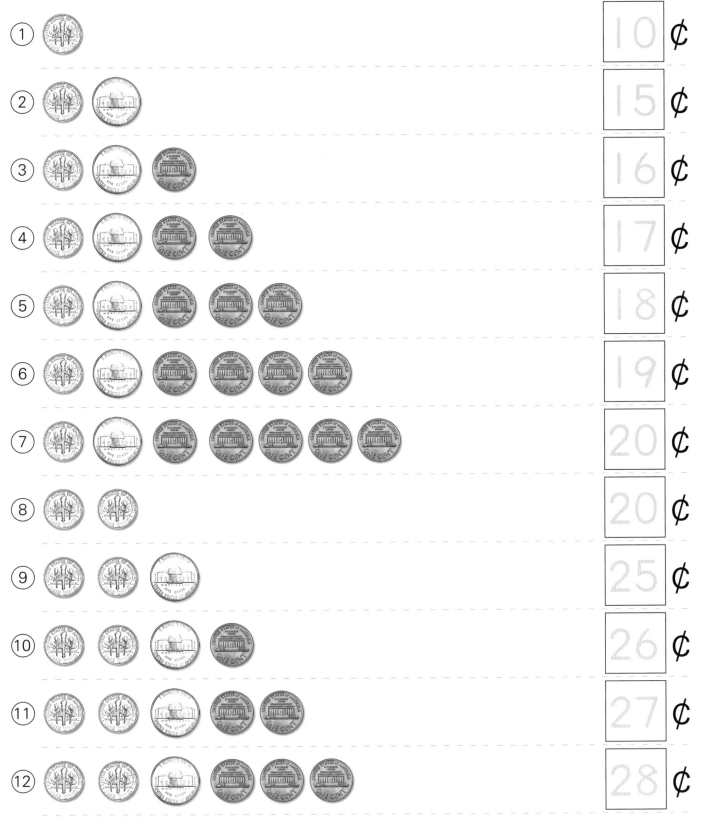

① 10 ¢

② 15 ¢

③ 16 ¢

④ 17 ¢

⑤ 18 ¢

⑥ 19 ¢

⑦ 20 ¢

⑧ 20 ¢

⑨ 25 ¢

⑩ 26 ¢

⑪ 27 ¢

⑫ 28 ¢

■ **Add the value of each row of coins. Then write the amount in the box on the right.**

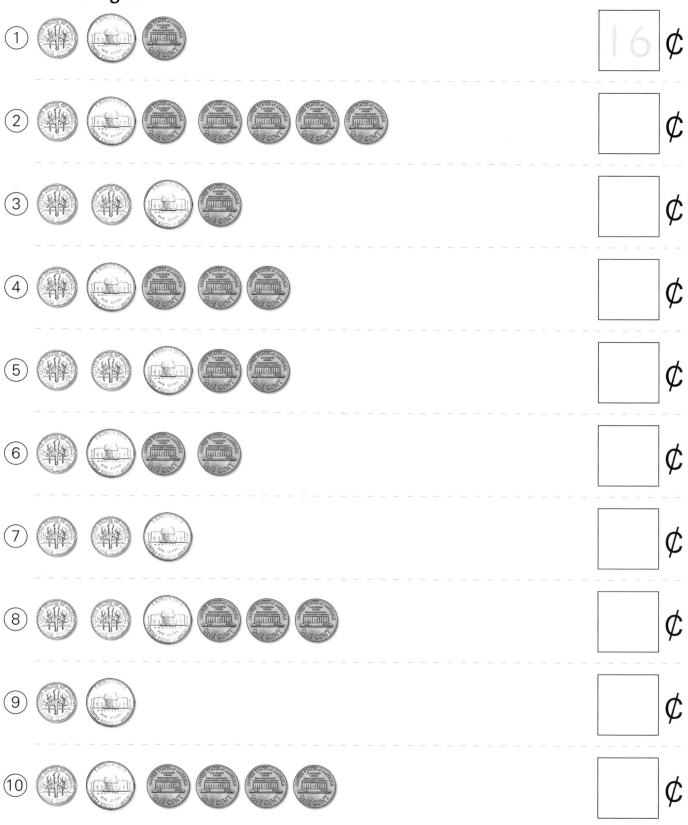

1. 16 ¢

2. ⬜ ¢

3. ⬜ ¢

4. ⬜ ¢

5. ⬜ ¢

6. ⬜ ¢

7. ⬜ ¢

8. ⬜ ¢

9. ⬜ ¢

10. ⬜ ¢

31 Counting Coins
Dimes, Nickels and Pennies

Name

Date

■ Add the value of each row of coins. Then trace the amount in the box on the right.

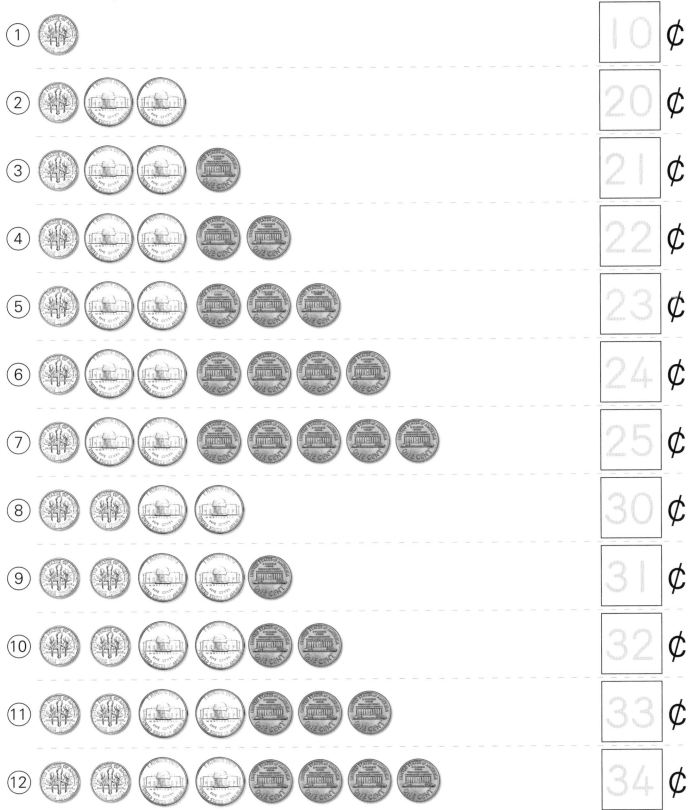

1. 10 ¢

2. 20 ¢

3. 21 ¢

4. 22 ¢

5. 23 ¢

6. 24 ¢

7. 25 ¢

8. 30 ¢

9. 31 ¢

10. 32 ¢

11. 33 ¢

12. 34 ¢

■ Add the value of each row of coins. Then write the amount in the box on the right.

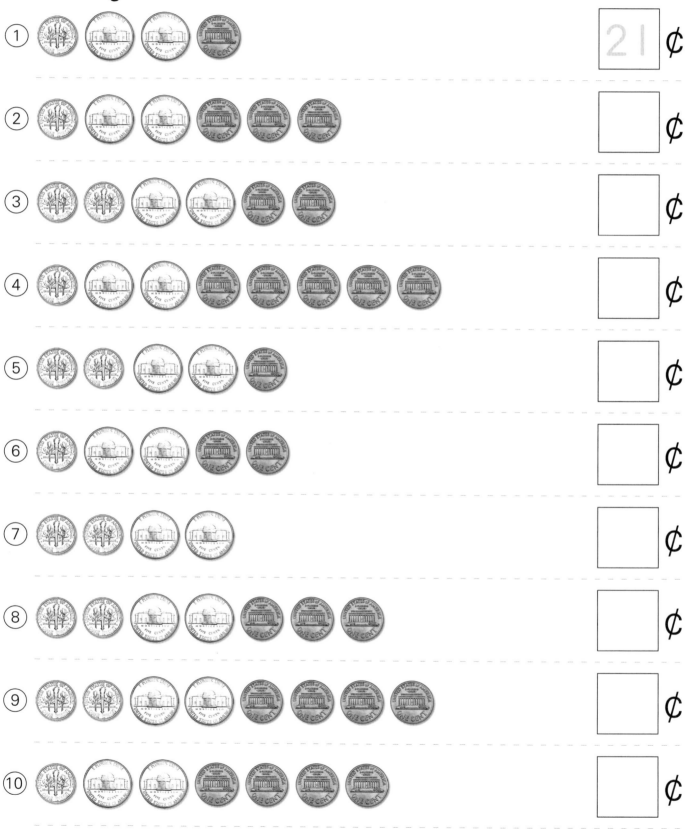

1. 21 ¢

2. ⬜ ¢

3. ⬜ ¢

4. ⬜ ¢

5. ⬜ ¢

6. ⬜ ¢

7. ⬜ ¢

8. ⬜ ¢

9. ⬜ ¢

10. ⬜ ¢

32 Counting Coins
Quarters, Nickels and Pennies

Name

Date

■ Add the value of each row of coins. Then trace the amount in the box on the right.

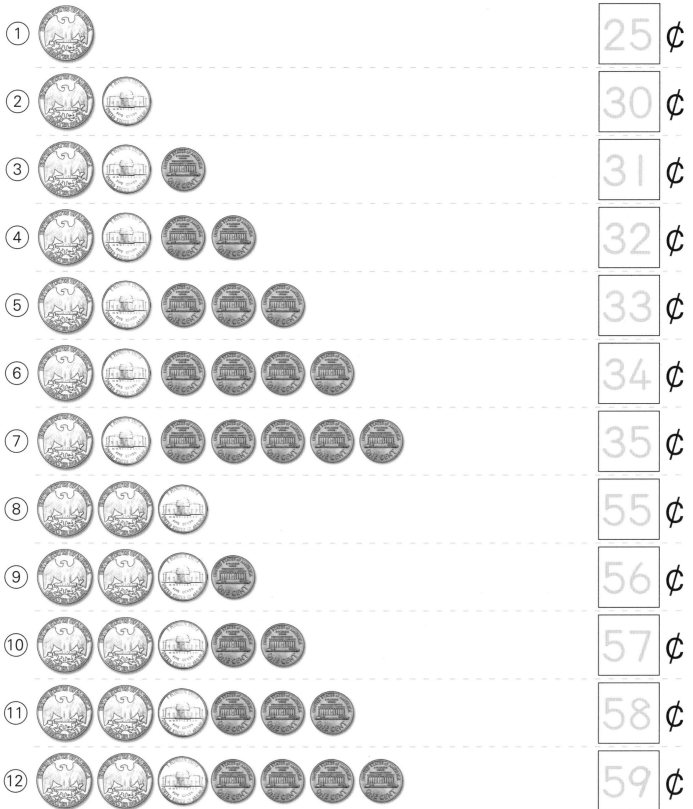

1. 25 ¢
2. 30 ¢
3. 31 ¢
4. 32 ¢
5. 33 ¢
6. 34 ¢
7. 35 ¢
8. 55 ¢
9. 56 ¢
10. 57 ¢
11. 58 ¢
12. 59 ¢

Add the value of each row of coins. Then write the amount in the box on the right.

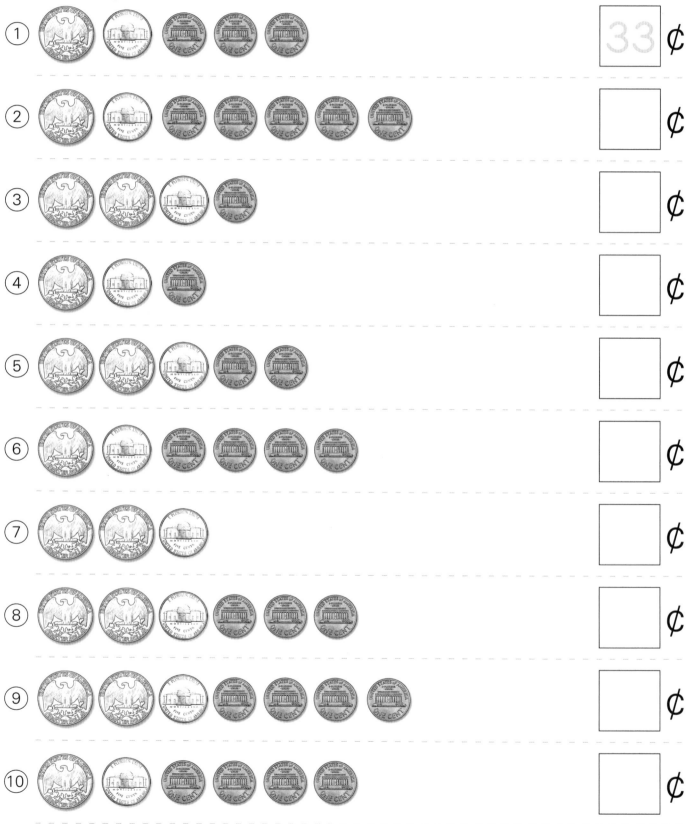

1. 33 ¢

2. ☐ ¢

3. ☐ ¢

4. ☐ ¢

5. ☐ ¢

6. ☐ ¢

7. ☐ ¢

8. ☐ ¢

9. ☐ ¢

10. ☐ ¢

Counting Coins
Quarters, Nickels and Pennies

Name

Date

■ Add the value of each row of coins. Then trace the amount in the box on the right.

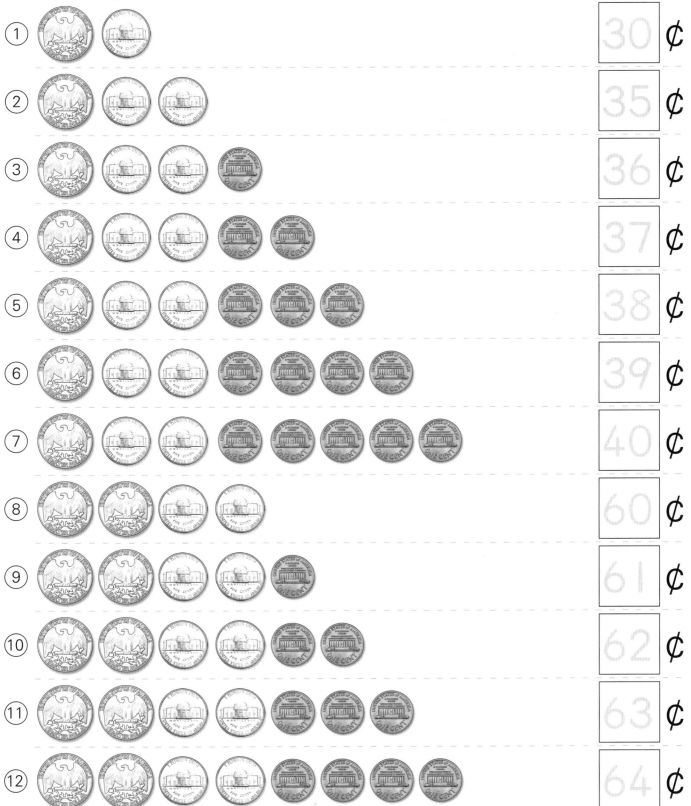

1. 30 ¢

2. 35 ¢

3. 36 ¢

4. 37 ¢

5. 38 ¢

6. 39 ¢

7. 40 ¢

8. 60 ¢

9. 61 ¢

10. 62 ¢

11. 63 ¢

12. 64 ¢

Add the value of each row of coins. Then write the amount in the box on the right.

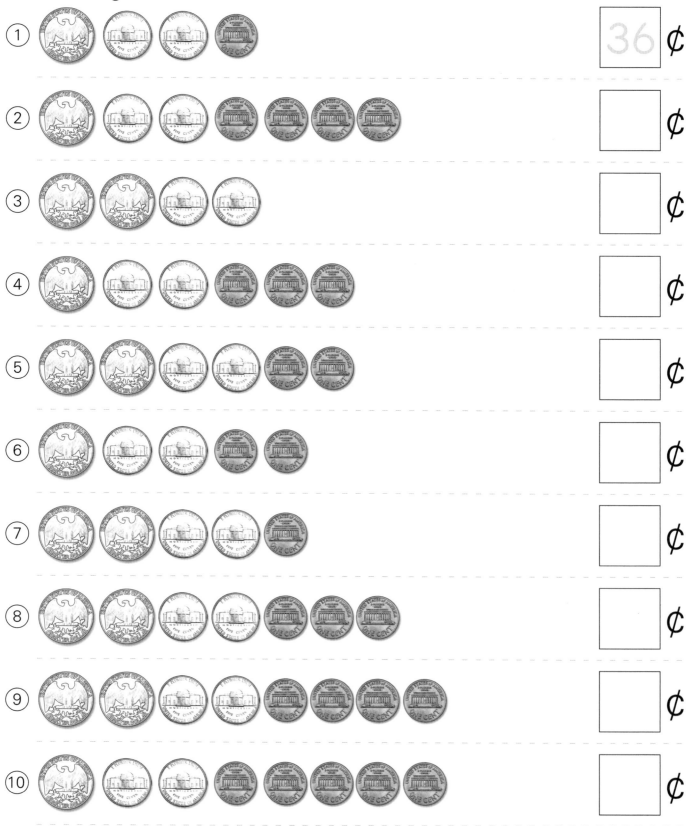

1. 36 ¢

2. ☐ ¢

3. ☐ ¢

4. ☐ ¢

5. ☐ ¢

6. ☐ ¢

7. ☐ ¢

8. ☐ ¢

9. ☐ ¢

10. ☐ ¢

Counting Coins
Quarters, Dimes and Pennies

■ Add the value of each row of coins. Then trace the amount in the box on the right.

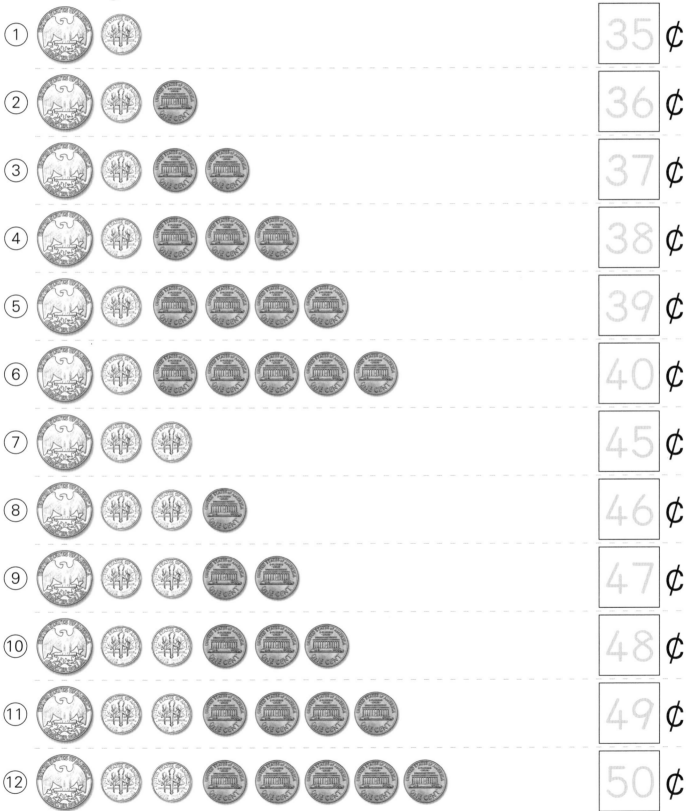

1. 35 ¢

2. 36 ¢

3. 37 ¢

4. 38 ¢

5. 39 ¢

6. 40 ¢

7. 45 ¢

8. 46 ¢

9. 47 ¢

10. 48 ¢

11. 49 ¢

12. 50 ¢

■ Add the value of each row of coins. Then write the amount in the box on the right.

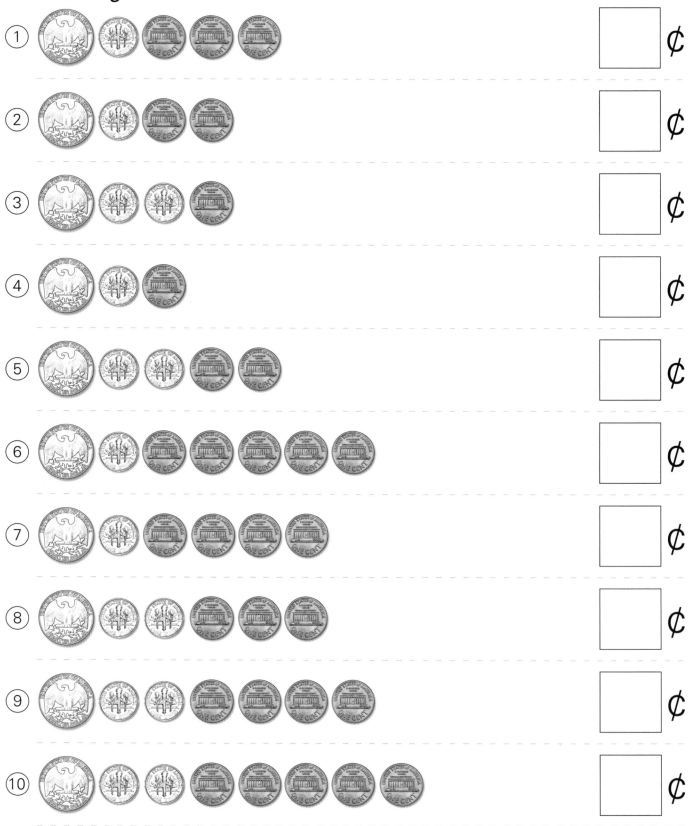

1. ☐ ¢

2. ☐ ¢

3. ☐ ¢

4. ☐ ¢

5. ☐ ¢

6. ☐ ¢

7. ☐ ¢

8. ☐ ¢

9. ☐ ¢

10. ☐ ¢

Review
How Much?

Name

Date

■ Add the value of the coins in each pocket. Then write the amount
in the box on the right.

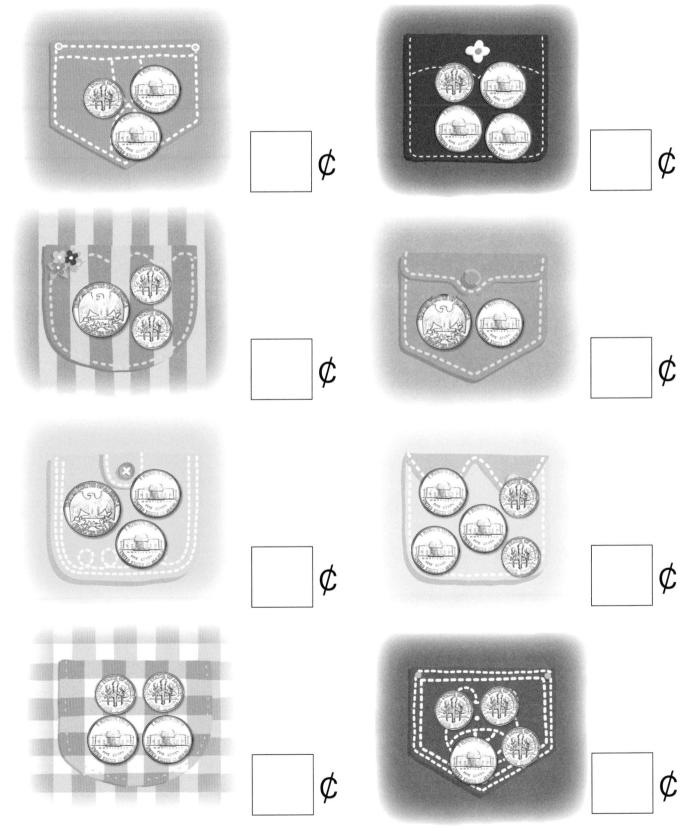

Add the value of the coins in each pocket. Then write the amount in the box on the right.

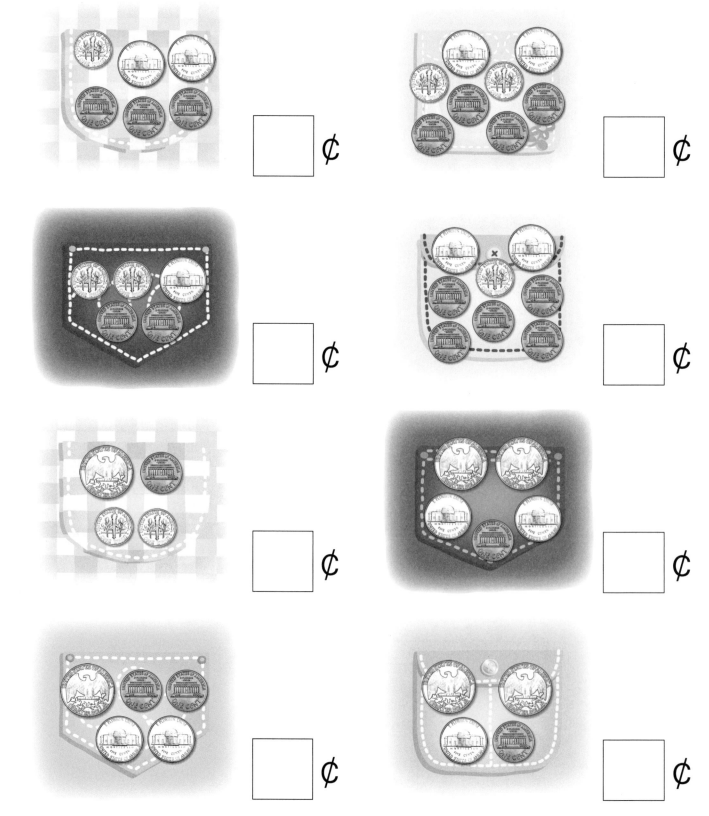

Counting Coins
Quarters, Dimes, Nickels and Pennies

To parents On this page, your child is asked to add the values of four different coins for the first time. Don't worry if your child struggles at first. Try the example with real coins until he or she understands.

■ Add the value of each row of coins. Then trace the amount in the box on the right.

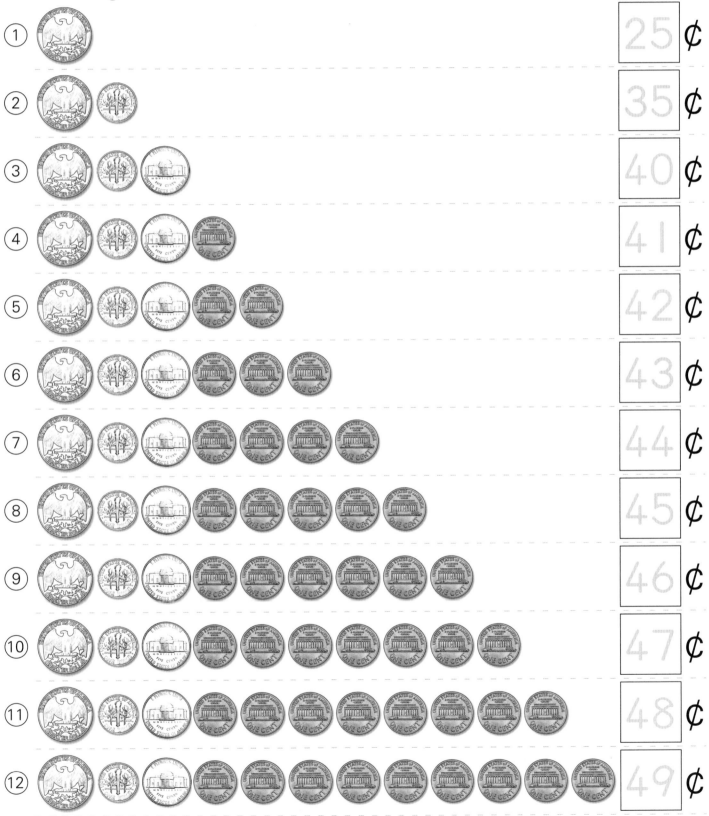

(1) 25 ¢

(2) 35 ¢

(3) 40 ¢

(4) 41 ¢

(5) 42 ¢

(6) 43 ¢

(7) 44 ¢

(8) 45 ¢

(9) 46 ¢

(10) 47 ¢

(11) 48 ¢

(12) 49 ¢

71

Add the value of each row of coins. Then write the amount in the box on the right.

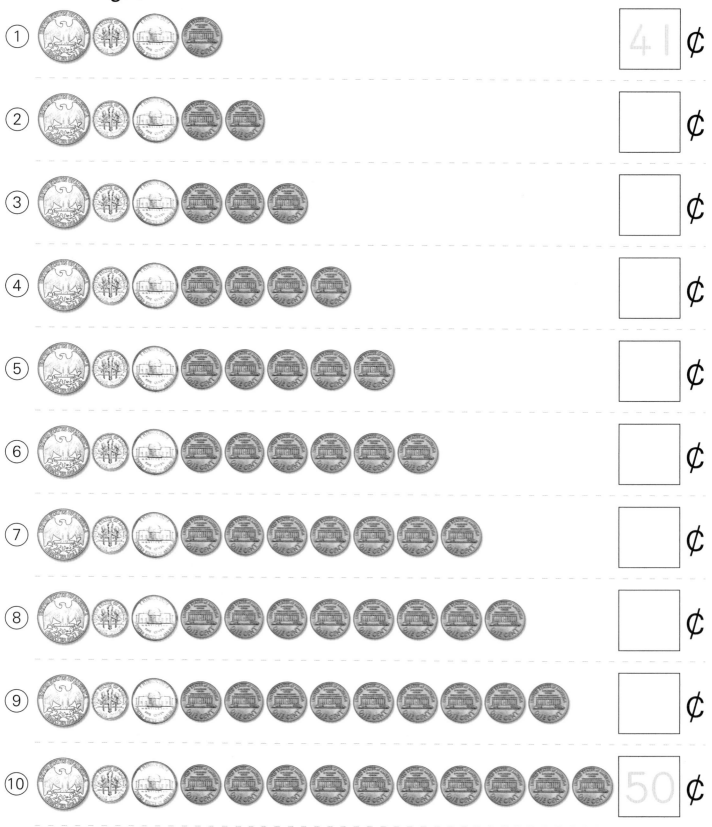

1. 41 ¢

2. ⬚ ¢

3. ⬚ ¢

4. ⬚ ¢

5. ⬚ ¢

6. ⬚ ¢

7. ⬚ ¢

8. ⬚ ¢

9. ⬚ ¢

10. 50 ¢

72

Counting Coins
Quarters, Dimes, Nickels and Pennies

■ Add the value of each row of coins. Then write the amount in the box on the right.

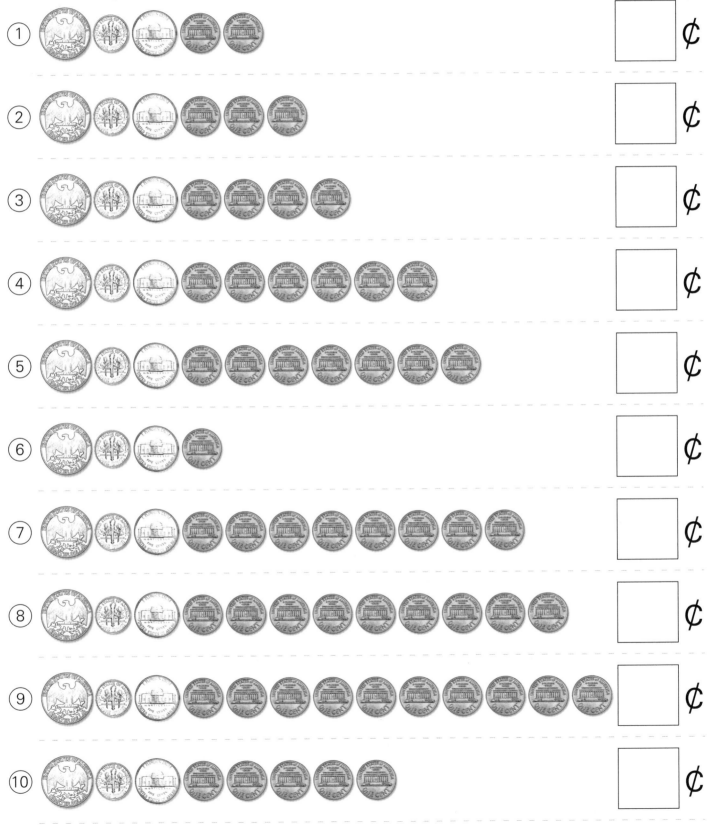

1. ☐ ¢

2. ☐ ¢

3. ☐ ¢

4. ☐ ¢

5. ☐ ¢

6. ☐ ¢

7. ☐ ¢

8. ☐ ¢

9. ☐ ¢

10. ☐ ¢

■ Add the value of each row of coins. Then write the amount in the box on the right.

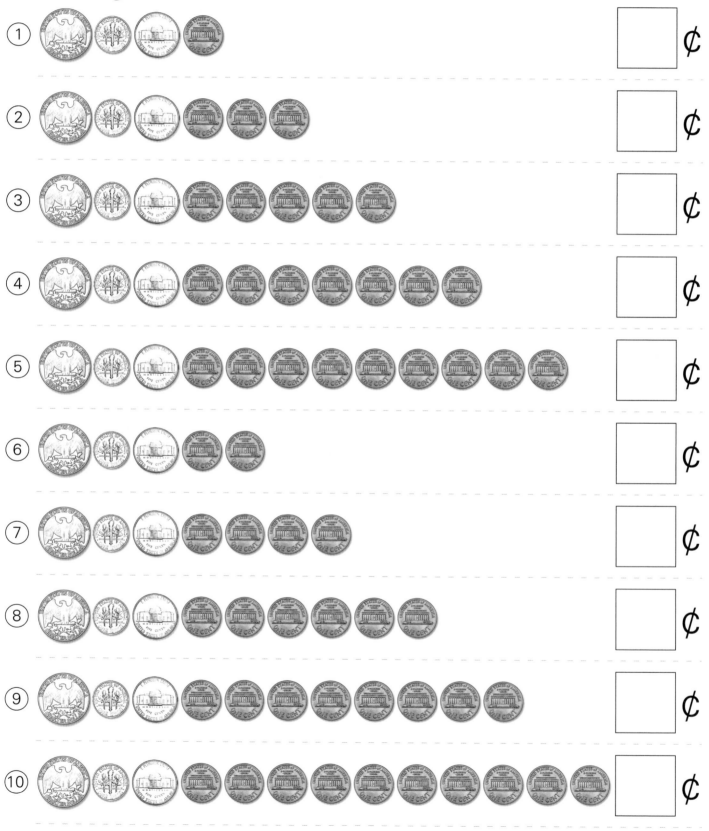

1. ☐ ¢

2. ☐ ¢

3. ☐ ¢

4. ☐ ¢

5. ☐ ¢

6. ☐ ¢

7. ☐ ¢

8. ☐ ¢

9. ☐ ¢

10. ☐ ¢

74

Counting Coins

Quarters, Dimes, Nickels and Pennies

Name

Date

■ Add the value of each row of coins. Then write the amount in the box on the right.

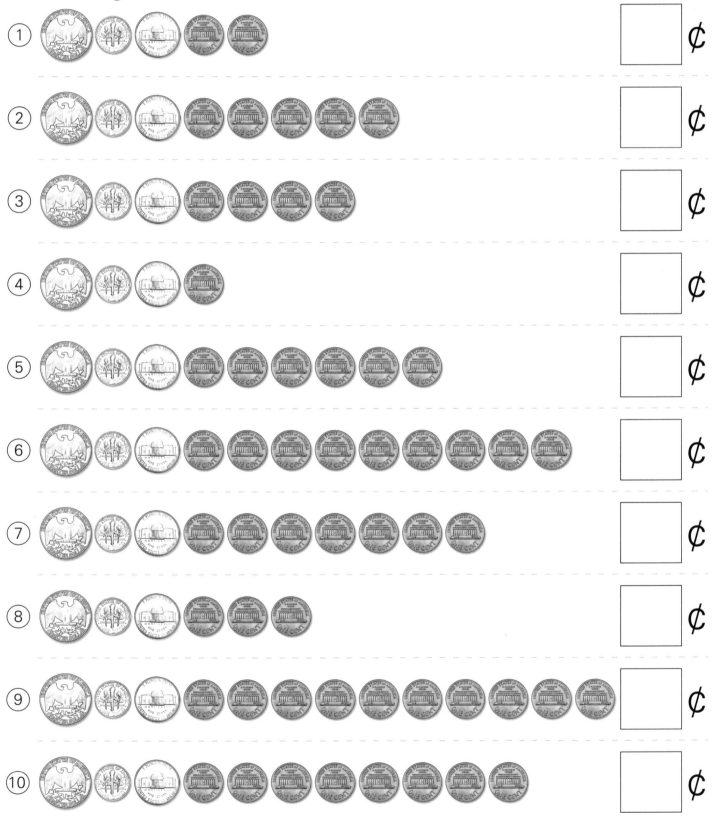

①   ¢

②   ¢

③   ¢

④   ¢

⑤   ¢

⑥   ¢

⑦   ¢

⑧   ¢

⑨   ¢

⑩   ¢

Add the value of each row of coins. Then write the amount in the box on the right.

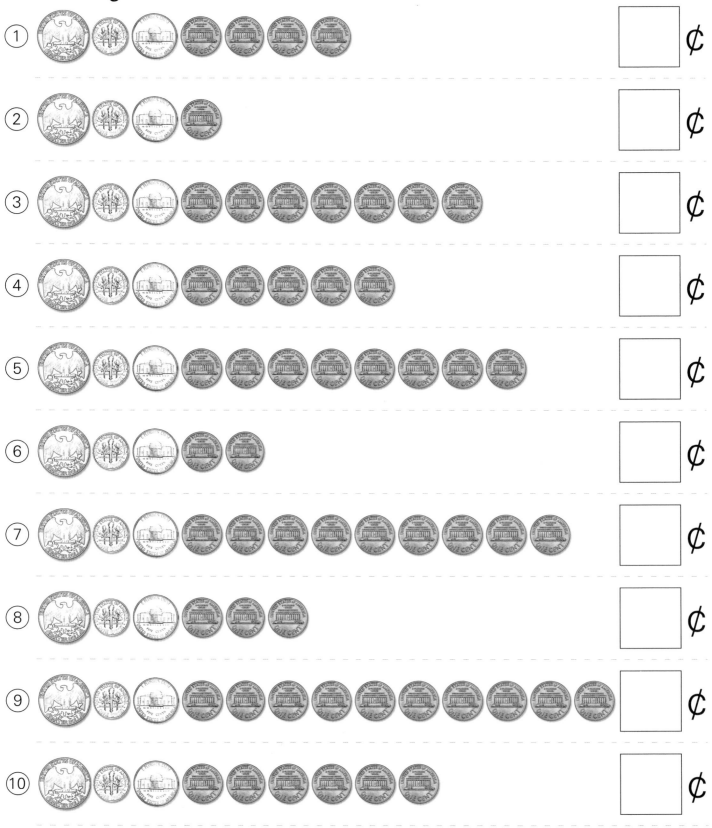

1.   ☐ ¢

2.   ☐ ¢

3.   ☐ ¢

4.   ☐ ¢

5.   ☐ ¢

6.   ☐ ¢

7.   ☐ ¢

8.   ☐ ¢

9.   ☐ ¢

10.   ☐ ¢

Review

How Much?

■ Add the value of the coins in each box. Then write the amount in the box on the right.

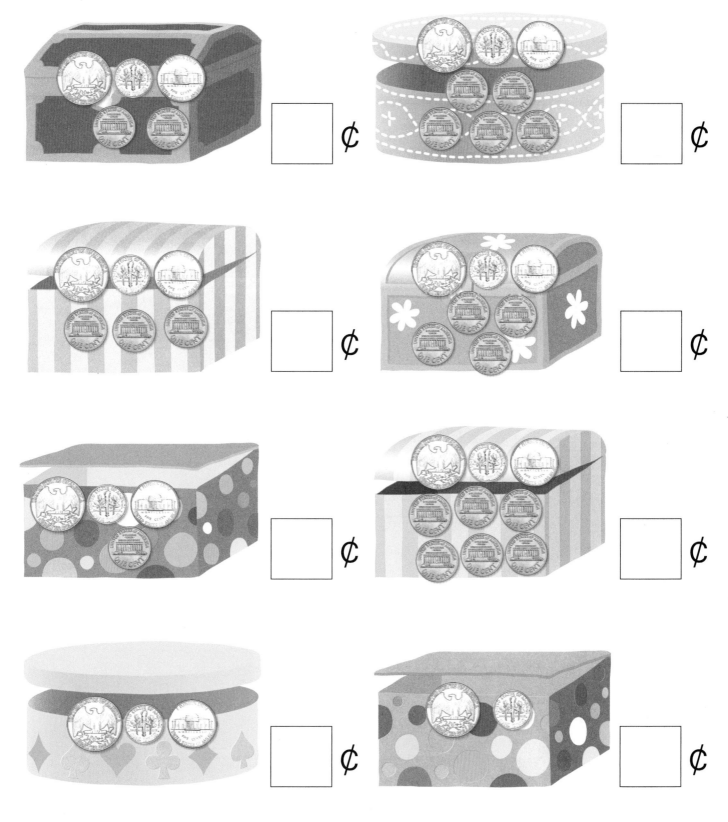

■Add the value of the coins in each box. Then write the amount in the box on the right.

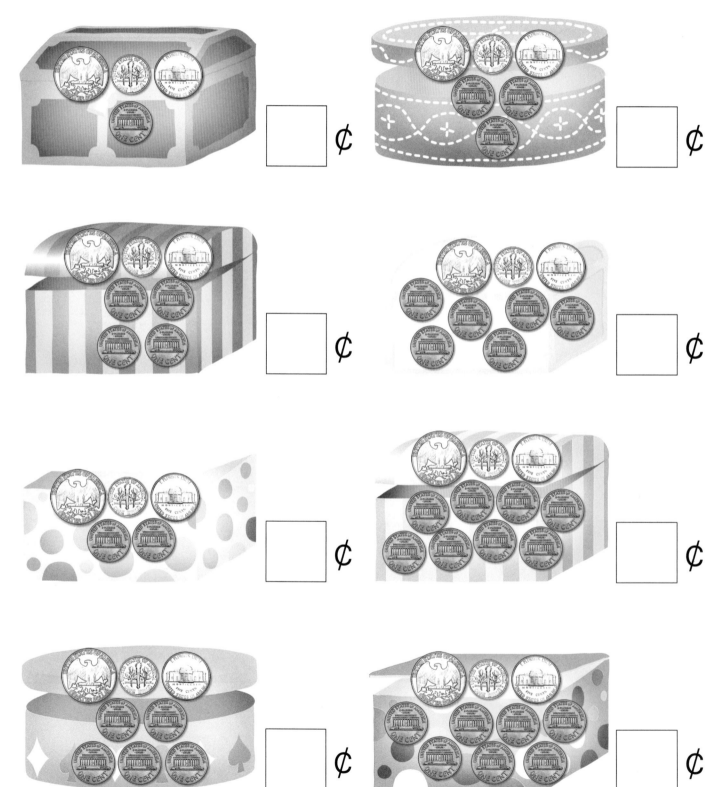

Review
How Much?

To parents Has your child enjoyed counting coins? Hopefully this workbook has helped him or her develop real-world math skills. Offer your child congratulations!

■ Add the value of the coins in each bank. Then write the amount in the box on the right.

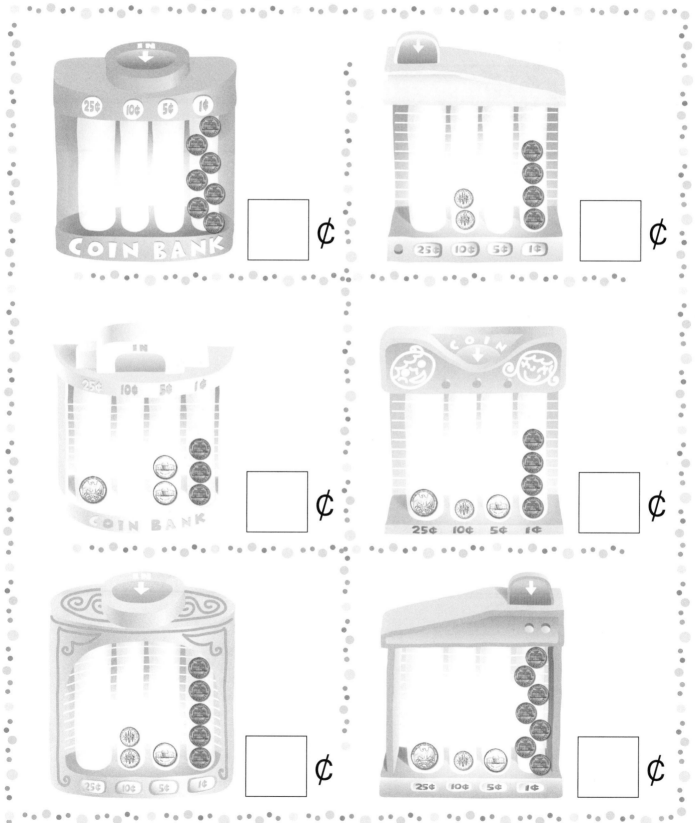

■Add the value of the coins in each cash register. Then write the amount in the box on the right.

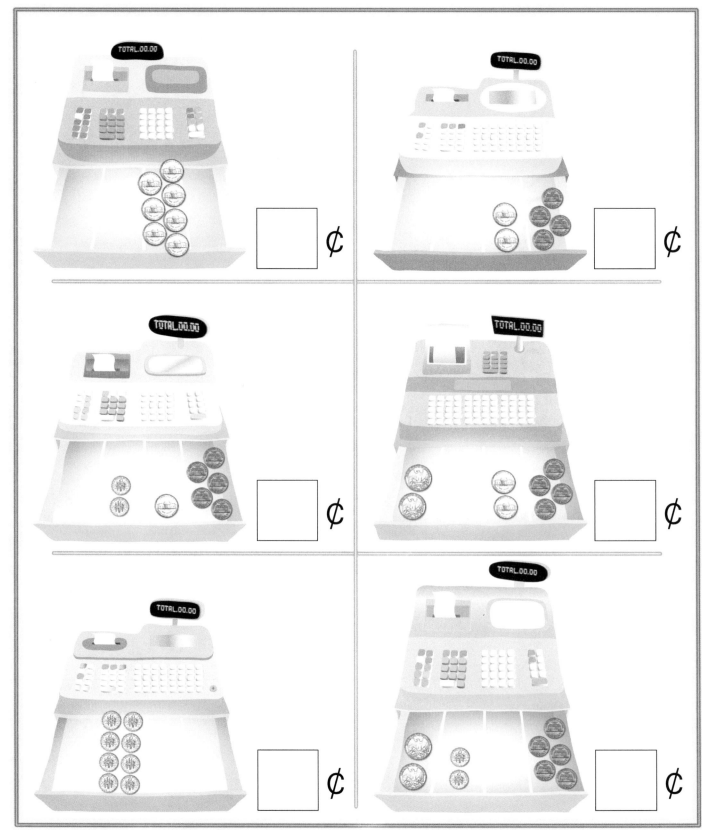

KUM⊙N

Certificate of Achievement

_____

is hereby congratulated on completing

My First Book of Money: Counting Coins

Presented on _____ , 20 _____

_____
Parent or Guardian